MORE
HAUNTED
HOOSIER
TRAILS

MORE

HAUNTED

HOOSIER

TRAILS

WANDA LOU WILLIS

CLERISY PRESS

Clerisy Press
306 Greenup Street
Covington, Kentucky 41011
clerisypress.com
A division of Keen Communications LLC

cover photo: Jonathan Tétrault
cover and book design: Kelly N. Kofron

Library of Congress Cataloging-in-Publication Data

Willis, Wanda Lou.
    More haunted Hoosier trails / by Wanda Lou Willis.
        p. cm.
    ISBN 978-1-57860-182-0
    1. Haunted places--Indiana. 2. Ghosts--Indiana. 3. Folklore--Indiana.
    I. Title.
    BF1472.U6W557 2004
    133.1'29772--dc22

                                                2004053330

For my parents, Ethel and Raymond Willis—
  I hear the mockingbird sing;
  The black-eyed china doll smiles;
  I am the keeper of the dream.

And for my brothers, Chester and Donald.

Those before, after, and always:
Beloved Angel and Dearest Joy.

Contents

NORTHERN INDIANA

16 BENTON
The Ghost of Justus Cemetery

20 ELKHART
A Tree with Spirit
Fun-Loving Nellie
Ghostly Good Samaritans
The Giant Ghost
The Haunting of Ruthmere Mansion
The Umble Ghost
The Weeping Tombstone

35 GRANT
Israel Jenkins House
The Phantom of the Opera House
The Spirit of Hostess House
The Ghosts of Mason's Bridge

46 JASPER
Moody Road Lights

51 LAGRANGE
She Still Waits

53 LAKE
The Ghosts of Cline Avenue
He's Still in the Game
Restless Spirits

61 MIAMI
On the Banks of the Wabash

64 NEWTON
Kentland Area Hauntings
70 PULASKI
The Praying Nun
72 TIPPECANOE
"Baby Alice"
White Wolf
78 WABASH
The Legend of Hanging Rock
Moonrock

CENTRAL INDIANA

86 BOONE
The Screaming Road
89 CLINTON
The "De-ghoster" Twins
The Ghosts of Sleepy Hollow
94 DELAWARE
Ball State Student Keeps Hanging Around
99 HOWARD
Jerome's Devil Dog
Kokomo's Haunted Funeral Home
108 MARION
Hannah House
House of Blue Lights
115 MONTGOMERY
The Devil's Creature
119 MORGAN
Gravity Hill
123 PUTNAM
Edna Collins Bridge

127 RANDOLPH
  The Ghost House
131 SHELBY
  The Blue River Concert
  The Enchanted Sisters
137 UNION
  The Spirit of Hanna House
  The Tilted Mill

SOUTHERN INDIANA

144 DAVIESS
  The Odon Fires
147 DECATUR
  The Friendly Ghost
  Greensburg Courthouse Ghost
152 GIBSON
  The Ghost of Cockrum Hall
  The Princeton Monster
157 JEFFERSON
  Haunted Hanover
161 JENNINGS
  Little Boy Lost
  Contrary Mary
167 MONROE
  The Ghosts of Indiana University
175 POSEY
  The Weeping Woman of Old Hoop-Pole Township
  Poseyville's Haunted Library
186 RIPLEY
  The Wolf Man

191 SPENCER
    The Mathias Sharp House
197 SULLIVAN
    The Ferree (Free) Springs Bridge Ghosts
200 VANDERBURGH
    Raining Stones
    Oscar the Friendly Ghost
    The Gray Lady of Willard Library

ACKNOWLEDGEMENTS

Throughout the process of researching, compiling, and writing this book, I was constantly reminded of the Hoosier warmth, friend-liness, and willingness to help others. A very special thanks to my friends for their support and encouragement: Eric Mundell, Jonathan Tétreault, Peggy McClelland, Ruth Harris, Ruth Holladay, Susan Richey, and Nelson Price.

Special recognition and thanks go to Joy, my Belgian shepherd, who, as always, was my confidant, my comfort, and my slave driver, unfailingly awakening me at two o'clock each morning and who throughout the many computer hours, stayed by my side.

My sincere thanks to the following people for supplying information on local ghost stories to supplement the hundreds of hours I spent in historical research among old newspapers and county histories; also, to those friends who were willing to provide photographs for the various stories:

Fun-Loving Nellie
> Jeanine Rhodes—Elkhart Public Library

A Tree with Spirit
> Marsha Eilers, Associate Director—Elkhart Public Library
> Linda Neff—Goshen Public Library
> Jeanine Rhodes—Elkhart Public Library

The Ghosts of Mason's Bridge
> Nancy Bryant, Director—Gas City-Mill Township Public Library
> Peggy Garrett, Executive Liaison—Gas City Area Chamber of Commerce

Israel Jenkins House
> Sara and Randy Ballinger, present owners

The Phantom of the Opera House
> Judy Cowling—Historic Fairmount, Inc.
> Cathy Shouse—*Chronicle T*
> Rhonda Stoffer, Head of Indiana History and Genealogy Services—Marion Public Library

The Spirit of Hostess House

Rhoda Stoffer, Head of Indiana History and Genealogy Services—Marion Public Library

On the Banks of the Wabash

Nancy Masten, Archivist—Miami County Museum

Kentland Area Hauntings

Kyle D. Conrad, informant

Matthew Havens, informant

Cheryl Wixon Gocken, President—Iroquois County, Ill. Genealogy Society

White Wolf

Robert C. Kriebel, Staff Reporter—*Lafayette Journal and C*

The Legend of Hanging Rock

Moonrock

Trula Frank, Executive Director—Wabash County Convention and Visitor's Bureau

Carolyn McNagny, Executive Director—Acres, Inc.

Davonne Rogers, Library Director—North Manchester Public Library

The "De-ghoster" Twins

Joan C. Bohm, Archivist, Genealogist—Clinton County Historical Society

Janis Thornton, Editor, Family—Frankfort *The Times*

Ball State Student Keeps Hanging Around

Mary Lou Gentis—Muncie Public library

Jerome's Devil Dog

Janice Blanchard—Howard County Public Library

Kokomo's Haunted Funeral Home

Tom Carey, Lifestyle Editor—Kokomo Þ

The Devil's Creature

Tracey Chapman Jones, informant

Judy Spencer—Crawfordsville Public Library

Judy Todd—Crawfordsville *The Weekly*

Edna Collins Bridge

Lou Fontaine—Putnam County Public Library

Susan Harmon, Local History Assistant—Putnam County Public Library

The Odon Fires

Catherine Hackett, Reference Librarian—Clark County Public Library, Springfield, Ohio

Joan Harvey, Library Services Supervisor—Indianapolis-Marion County Public Library

The Friendly Ghost
Greensburg Courthouse Ghost
   Vicki Butz—Greensburg Public Library
   Kathie Scheidler—Greensburg Public Library
   Pat Smith, Columnist—*Greensburg Daily News*
Poseyville's Haunted Library
   Stanley Melburn Campbell, Director—Poseyville Public Library
The Weeping Woman of Old Hoop-Pole Township
   Steve Cochran, Director—Alexandrian Public Library
   Becca Goldman, Head of Community Relations—Alexandrian Public Library
   Marissa Priddis, Assistant Director—Alexandrian Public Library
The Wolf Man
   Bill Poor, Director—Tyson Library
   Jeremy Sobecki, Assistant Manager—Versailles State Park
The Mathias Sharp House
   Vevah Harris—Spencer County Visitor's Bureau
   Becky Middleton—Spencer County Public Library
The Ferree (Free) Springs Bridge Ghosts
   Rebecca Cole—Sullivan Public Library
Oscar the Friendly Ghost
   Sue Thomas—Evansville Public Library
The Gray Lady of Willard Library
   Greg Hager, Director—Willard Library
   Patricia Sides, Archivist—Willard Library

NORTHERN
INDIANA

BENTON COUNTY

❖❖❖❖❖❖❖❖❖❖ BENTON COUNTY, a part of Indiana's vast grand prairie, was organized in 1840 and named for Missouri politician Thomas Hart Benton. No commissioners were appointed, and it was not until 1843 that a county seat was selected.

The first county seat, Oxford, was platted in 1843. Within one year of the town's establishment, it had gone through three name changes. It was first called Milroy after one of the original founders, then Hartford after the Connecticut city; however, when it was discovered that both these names were already being used by other counties, it was renamed Oxford.

It's not clear why this name was chosen—perhaps for the English city and university—although one legend says the name was chosen for the many oxen-driven wagons that forded nearby Pine Creek. In 1873 the county courthouse was condemned and the seat of government moved to Fowler.

A New England land speculator, Henry L. Ellsworth purchased nearly ninety thousand acres of Benton County. Other New Englanders followed suit, including Noah and Daniel Webster and members of Boston's Cabot family. Ellsworth bequeathed most of his land to Yale University.

After the land speculators, the cattle barons moved in. Moses Fowler's twenty-thousand-acre cattle farm was the home to one of the largest herds. His brother-in-law, Adams Earl, established America's foundation herd of imported, purebred Herefords.

The cattle barons lent their names to many of the communities throughout the county: Fowler, Earl Park, Raub, Atkinson, Boswell, Chase, and Templeton.

The tiny settlement of Wadena produced a record number of baseball players in the early 1900s. Fred (Cy) Williams (1889–1974) twice led the National League in home runs. He was the first player in the majors to ever hit more than two hundred home runs. In 1923 he tied with Babe Ruth for the most home runs hit that season. His all-time batting average stands at .292.

Pitcher Otis Crandall (1887–1951) was christened "Doc" when Damon Runyan joked that he was "the physician of the pitching emergency." Doc Crandall, considered the best relief pitcher of his era, had a .623 lifetime win percentage in the National and Federal leagues. Crandall's two brothers played in the American Association and International leagues.

Perhaps the most famous son of Benton County was Dan Patch—a horse (1896–1916). The famed horse was born at Kelly's Livery Stable in Oxford on Indiana 352, im-mediately south of Indiana 55. The white barn on the left is easily distinguished by the words "Dan Patch 1:55" spelled out on the green shingled roof. His first owner, Dan Mess-ner, was a local merchant. His trainer, John Wattles, was also a local man. During his career Dan Patch had two other owners: M.E. Sturgis of New York (1901–1902) and M.W. Savage of Minneapolis, Minnesota (1902–1916).

At four years old, Dan Patch began his legendary racing career. Until he stopped competitive racing in 1909, he won every race except two, in which he finished second. Because of lack of competition, Dan Patch raced in exhibitions against the clock, and in 1905 he set the world's record for the mile with the time of one minute, fifty-five seconds—a record that stood for thirty-three years.

Although "Patch," as he was fondly known, was a classic racing horse in terms of beauty and grace, the trotter seemed to have almost human characteristics. He was gentle, easy to handle, and was said to recognize friends and understand what was said to him. He always seemed willing to please and often played the showman to the crowds. He was as gentle as a Newfoundland dog.

After competing in the 1901 Grand Circuit, Dan Patch returned to Oxford on November 2, 1901, a day designated as Dan Patch Day that is still celebrated more than one hundred years later.

Dan Patch died in 1916, preceding his owner, Savage, in death by only one day. ❖

The Ghost of Justus Cemetery

The clouds scurried across the night sky, at times hiding the pale moonlight. It was a windy, chilly, rainy night, not a good night for man or beast to venture out—a perfect night for ghosts.

It was the era of the steam engine, and a train traveling on the Chicago & Eastern Illinois Railroad stopped at the Oxford, Indiana, water tower located within view of the Justus Cemetery. As the crewmembers began taking on water above the whine of the wind, they heard distinctly a mournful moaning. Passengers hearing the sound strained their eyes into the darkness trying to learn from where and what this sound was coming.

Suddenly a figure in white was seen floating from the cemetery through the air toward the idle train. Its moans could be heard above the wind. The crewmembers and passengers watched, frozen with fright. Women began screaming. The crewmembers worked frantically to complete the task of taking on water. Suddenly without warning the specter retreated back to the cemetery, plunging headlong into an open grave.

The crewmembers were understandably frightened. Some even asked for transfers to daylight trains or better still, to any other train that did not have to pass through Oxford—and the Justus Cemetery.

Once again, a few nights later, the train made its customary and needed stop at the Oxford water tower. The crew had completed the task when the ghost appeared. The train began to get up a head of steam but was unable to move for several minutes, its wheels spinning on the track. The crewmembers became nearly hysterical when suddenly with a jerk the train began to roll free from whatever horror had held it tight in its grasp. Fear and panic consumed the crew, and with open defiance, the train's crew refused to take the train into Oxford on its next run. Railroad officials were at a loss to know what to do and finally hired a detective.

After visiting Oxford and talking to some of the citizens, he was able to persuade a few to accompany him one night as he visited the cemetery. This was scary business he was proposing. As the small group waited and watched, they observed some of the young men of the community creep into the area just before the train arrived to take on water. One of them carried something white—a sheet. The detective left his hiding place, and the others followed as he approached the young men. The youthful pranksters admitted they were responsible for the ghost. They had attached a wire from the top of the water tower to the cemetery and were pulling a sheet, draped over a coat hanger, along this "track." They also confessed that they had rubbed soap on the railroad tracks to make it difficult for the train to get traction once it had stopped. The pranksters were set free with a stern warning that if this ever happened again they would be arrested.

That ended the life of the ghost of Justus Cemetery—or did it? There were some among the train's crew—those who had been frightened into near hysterics—who didn't believe that it was a prank.

ELKHART COUNTY

❖❖❖❖❖❖❖❖❖❖❖ ORGANIZED IN 1830, Elkhart County and the city of Elkhart were both named for the Elkhart River. The Potawatomi named the river for an island at the confluence of the Elkhart and Saint Joseph Rivers, which according to legend the Indians thought resembled an elk's heart.

Oliver Crane began platting Goshen, the county seat, in 1831. According to one local tradition, Crane chose to name the city after his hometown, Goshen, in Orange County, New York. However, another tradition states the land was rich and productive, like the biblical Goshen, and thus the city was named for the biblical land.

Goshen College, a private preparatory school, was founded in 1894 by the Mennonite Church and was originally called the Elkhart Institute of Science, Industry, and the Arts. The institution moved to its present campus in 1903, where it became an accredited four-year liberal arts school and changed its name to Goshen College. Still owned by the Mennonite Church, Goshen College continues to expand; one of its newest additions is the John S. Umble Center for the Performing Arts. In 1980 Goshen became the first American undergraduate school to negotiate a four-teen-week educational exchange with a college in China.

Elkhart city, located on the south side of Elkhart River, was platted by Dr. Havilah Beardsley in 1832. Elkhart was incorporated as a town in 1858 and a city in 1875. Beardsley's wife, Rachael Calhoun Beardsley, was said to have been a cousin to Vice President John Calhoun.

Until the railroad arrived in 1851, the city was an active river port, shipping flour, pork, and other produce to Lake Michigan.

Elkhart city also boasts a rich musical history—one that began when a cornet player, C.G. Conn, injured his lip. As a result of this injury, Conn invented the rubber mouthpiece. He began selling them in 1873. This sparked Elkhart's musical instrument industry, which led to the city being known as "The band capital of the world." At one time there were eleven Elkhart factories manufacturing band instruments. Today there are approximately eight involved in the manufacturing of woodwinds, brass instruments, and pianos.

At one time Elkhart manufactured more than twenty makes of automobile, second in the state only to Indianapolis. Elkhart is also known as the "recreational vehicle capital of the world," with approximately two hundred firms manufacturing mobile homes, campers, or other recreational vehicle-related products.

Another Elkhart resident who would become notorious, Dr. Franklin Miles began marketing his home remedy, a sedative known as Dr. Miles's Restorative Nervine, in 1884. The company achieved fame in the 1930s as the producer of Alka-Seltzer. Several years later One-A-Day vitamins and S.O.S steel wool pads were added to its product line. Miles Laboratory since has been purchased by Bayer AG of West Germany, the developer of Bayer aspirin. The billion-dollar, high-tech Miles Laboratory headquarters are still located in Elkhart.

In front of the Greek Revival-style courthouse at the northwest corner of Main Street and Lincoln Avenue sits an octagonal limestone structure. Built by the Work Progress Administration (WPA), the structure was erected across the street from the town's bank—a highly guarded location following the notorious Dillinger gang's widely publicized bank robberies in neighboring cities. The police manned the bullet-proof enclosure around the clock from 1939 to 1969.

The 155-acre Bonneyville Mill County Park is of historical interest. The state's oldest continuously operated gristmill is located here. In 1832 Edward Bonney constructed a dam on the Little Elkhart River and erected the water-powered mill. The Bonney Mill is listed on the National Register of Historic Places.

Bonney led a colorful life. He was arrested in 1842 for counterfeiting. He managed to escape from prison, and he and his family moved near the Mormon community of Nauvoo, Illinois.

In a published autobiographical account of his life, *The Banditti of the Prairies or The Murderer's Doom: A Tale of the Mississippi Valley*, he told of working for the Pinkerton Detective Agency. During his tenure there, he led a thirteen-month chase after nine thieves and murderers across a four-state area. He also served in the 127th Illinois infantry during the Civil War. After his death in 1863 at age fifty-nine, his body was returned for burial near the mill. ❖

A Tree with Spirit

A few miles southwest of Elkhart on County Road 19 is the village of Jimtown (Jamestown). It was laid out in 1835 by James Davis, for whom it was named. The village has remained just that—a village—a quiet and comfortable place to live. Like in many other small communities, everybody knows everybody. In such a peaceful environment, a visitor passing through would feel certain there was nothing to fear. But those who live in and near the community know the truth.

Some time back, a terrible auto accident occurred just west of Jimtown on Cable Line Road (County Road 26). The driver died on the spot. No one recalls the exact date of the accident or even the name of the driver, but nearly everyone in the area agrees the accident did happen. It left a legacy—a terrible legacy.

As the story is often told, it began on a moonless night. A cold mist hugged the ground. An eastbound car traveling much too fast on County Road 26 was nearing the intersection at County Road 11. Suddenly the driver lost control. The vehicle crashed headlong into a large tree just off the side of the road. On impact, the driver was thrown through the windshield, crashing into the tree.

A nearby family heard the crash and called the sheriff's office. People watching the wreckage cleanup commented that they could see the exact spot where the man's body had hit the tree. Curiously, his body was never found.

Some believed he had survived the crash and in shock had wandered into the woods where he died. Others had a different theory. They believed the force of the impact was so great that the tree had actually captured the man's body—and his spirit!

As time passed the tree became diseased and was cut down. The road, however, is still haunted. Today, the thing that remains to haunt Cable Line Road is said to be a monster.

Traveling at night, you may see in your headlights the man's head floating above the road searching for its body or a headless creature standing at the edge of the road.

The legend has been so much a part of Jimtown's culture that when the town celebrated its 150-year anniversary, the Cable Line Monster was honored with its own float!

Fun-Loving Nellie

A lively and fashionable young woman, devoted to her family and husband, Nellie Knickerbocker, daughter of Mr. and Mrs. Charles Winchester, was said to be the subject of more talk than anyone who ever lived in Elkhart. Although she's been dead for nearly fifty years, she's still the topic of conversation. There is "evidence" that she possibly still exists—at least on some level.

When William H. Knickerbocker met the diminutive blue-eyed beauty he fell in love. Although he was ten years older, Nellie's father gave them his blessings. They were married on November 29, 1882.

Charles Winchester built a mansion at 517 South Second Street where the Winchesters and Knickerbockers lived together. At the time it was considered one of the best-built homes in the city. Air spaces between the inner and outer walls acted as insulation against outside noises.

The couple hosted many lavish parties with Nellie, a talented pianist, entertaining the guests. She was a very modern and independent young lady. The petite Nellie was often seen driving her 1914 electric Milburn around town.

For Nellie, however, it wasn't all parties, music, and driving about town. There were times of sadness and desolate loneliness. Nellie and William had one son, Howard, who died in infancy. Shortly afterward, she lost her father and, then her mother passed away. Ultimately, Nellie was left completely alone when her husband passed away four years later.

During the years before her own death, she became a reclusive eccentric. She no longer drove her beloved Milburn. Her chauffeur would drive her to the Hotel Elkhart where she'd have her meals. She was known to the staff for her generous tips.

As the years passed, she adopted what some called a "fetish" about cemeteries. She spent a great deal of time at Grace Lawn Cemetery tending the family plot. She became obsessed with her own burial arrangements. She wanted to make sure her coffin was as good as her parents' and husband's. Afraid her surviving relatives (her husband's nieces) would slight her in death and bury her in a cheap coffin, she purchased a seamless, solid copper casket and stored it in her dining room.

Stories about the coffin began circulating around Elkhart. It was said Nellie actually slept or at least rested in it to be certain that she would be comfortable during her eternal rest. Although this was a popular belief, no one knew for certain. In 1944 the house was sold to a couple from Goshen, with the understanding that Nellie could remain there until her death.

In 1947 Nellie died—alone. Her house attendant found her sitting in a chair. Again the rumors circulated. Some believed she was found lying inside the coffin, waiting for the undertaker.

Private services were attended by some of the bank's directors, a few friends, and the waitresses from Hotel Elkhart. She was buried at Grace Lawn Cemetery beside her parents, son, and husband with a mammoth concrete cross towering over the site.

She had been the daughter and wife of prosperous businessmen, and yet her estate amounted to only $11,000. What had happened to the Knickerbocker fortune?

Shortly after her death, court and bank officials searched the home. Carpeting was removed. Even the spaces between the walls were searched. Neither money nor family documents were ever found.

The Goshen family lived in Nellie's home for several uneventful years before leasing it to the Juhl Advertising Agency. A reporter for the *Elkhart Truth* asked several Juhl employees if they thought Nellie was still in the house. The question was answered by guarded laughter. Over the years, the employees had adopted a habit of half-heartedly blaming Nellie for any inexplicable happenings.

One employee commented, "If she exists, as a ghost, she's fairly benign." However, he admitted to being one of the first to have had an inexplicable experience. He was taking some friends through the mansion when the back of a grandfather clock fell out. No one had been near it, nor had there been a sonic boom, earth-moving equipment in use, or a tremor. Of course, Nellie got the blame.

Another strange happening occurred in a room that was being used to store magazines. Instead of the stacks growing, they seemed to be getting smaller. Later the magazines were found in the basement just below a laundry chute that began in this room. Some of the employees believed the fun-loving Nellie was still enjoying a joke from time to time.

Another employee admitted to the reporter that he'd experienced several bizarre events. The most bizarre of these happened during the Christmas season. He was walking past the office's Christmas tree when suddenly it toppled over and fell on him! Again, no one had been around the tree, and there was no explanation—other than Nellie.

In another of the man's stories, he was by himself working after hours in the conference room when all of a sudden a gust of wind scattered the papers he was working on. He wouldn't have thought anything of it—if the windows and doors hadn't been shut!

The employees also told of recurring strange experiences with a storage closet door. The door was secured by a latch that required a firm tug to open. Yet, employees were forever going to the room and finding the door open.

Another employee recounted experiences from an evening spent alone in the house with his young daughter. The girl insisted she heard something like money jingling. In an effort to quiet her fears, they looked around for the source but found no one in the building or anything unusual. A short time later, she tugged at her father's arm, this time saying she heard footsteps on the stairs to the attic. At that point, her father decided it was time to leave.

Today, Nellie's home, which has suffered from a lack of loving human occupants, will be getting a new lease on life. The newly created Winchester Group is planning to undertake its restoration. Once this has been done, the second floor of the building will be available for offices. The first floor will maintain the historical presence of the structure—and the entire home, perhaps, its ghostly presence.

Ghostly Good Samaritans

In 1984 the *Elkhart Truth* retold a story of two women who were driving alone on a road at night. They were just north of South Bend, but below the Michigan state line. They'd lost their way and didn't even know what road they were on. As they came to a hill, the car stalled. They tried and tried to get the motor to turn over, but with no success.

There wasn't a house in sight. In fact, there weren't any lights anywhere. A sense of isolation and fear came over the women. As they sat there trying to decide what to do, two strangers appeared. Cautiously, the driver rolled her window down just enough to ask if the two men would help them.

They nodded and began pushing the car slowly up the hill. As it reached the peak, it began rolling quickly down the other side. Once sufficient speed was reached, the driver was able to get the engine to turn over.

The women were so grateful they turned the car around to go back and thank the good Samaritans. When they returned to the spot where the car had died, no one was around. Both of the women got out of the car and began calling out, hoping the men would hear them and return to receive their grateful thanks. No one answered. There was only silence in the night. As the women turned to go back to their car, they stood in amazement.

The car, which had been left idling, was once again making that slow ascent up the hill as if it were being pushed. The women be-gan running, reaching the car just before it arrived at the top of the hill. They opened the doors and jumped in. The driver put her foot on the gas pedal and kept right on going—never stopping and never looking back until they'd reached their destination.

They were convinced that the two men were ghostly good Samaritans, standing watch over the hill, waiting to help unfortunate motorists with a push up the hill.

The Giant Ghost

The story of the giant ghost of Benton in Elkhart County became a news item in the September 13, 1896, issue of the *Philadelphia Press*.

The story attracted so much attention that many upstanding, intelligent individuals who were considered to have good sense decided to investigate.

This is the story as it was reported: A farmer and his wife were returning home one night from a visit with one of their neighbors. The road to their farm, about sixteen miles southeast of Elkhart, passed near an old church surrounded by a moss-covered, overgrown graveyard.

For years, an old man who lived not far from the graveyard had tended to the gravesites, keeping the vegetation under control. Ten years before, however, the old man was found murdered. He had been beaten to death by a large club, which was found beside his cold body. The motive for this dastardly deed was the rumored hoard of gold he supposedly had hidden. The crime was never solved.

The old man was buried in the graveyard where he'd spent so much of his time. Sadly, after his death no one continued to maintain the hallowed ground and final resting places of the county's pioneer families.

This particular night, as the farmer and his wife neared the graveyard, the horses reared back on their haunches, eyes bulging, ears flicking as they snorted in terror. The farmer was alarmed and suspected the horses had gotten the scent of highwaymen hiding in the shadows. He reached for a shotgun laying in the bottom of the wagon for just such an emergency. His wife screamed. She pointed straight ahead, grabbing his arm speechlessly.

Blocking their way, standing in the road just beside the old graveyard, was an apparition of a man with a long white beard sweeping over his chest. The man had to be no less than eight feet tall. In one of his hands, he carried a large club similar to the one that had been used ten years earlier to kill the old cemetery caretaker.

Slowly raising his free arm, the ghost bowed and, with a majestic sweep of his arm, beckoned the farmer to come ahead. The farmer struggled to restrain the panicked horses while his wife sat beside him, dumbstruck and frozen with fear.

The farmer, still struggling with his team, watched in apprehension and mounting fear as the ghostly figure slowly began to move toward the wagon. The large club was now raised to its shoulder, much as a soldier would carry his rifle. The farmer saw that the fearsome figure moved without touching the ground—just floating above the road.

Whirling his team around, the farmer lashed the horses into a run, racing back toward the house of the friend he had just left. The next day in broad daylight the couple once again began their trip home—this time completing their journey without incident.

Shortly thereafter another farmer in the area encountered the giant ghost. This man had a reputation for being not only intelligent, but without fear. His encounter with the giant club-wielding ghost, however, left him greatly fearful. He never again traveled that road at night.

On a number of occasions, several groups of curious citizens have attempted to investigate and solve the mystery of the giant ghost. In each instance they, too, saw and were convinced of the actual presence of the ghost.

Several conflicting reports described the ghost as being eight to ten feet tall and having a badly mangled or missing head. But all the reports mentioned the club. The story evolved to allege that the entity was the spirit of the elderly man who must have been murdered by a gang of gold-seeking ruffians. Some said that the ghost would not hurt the innocent; he was just waiting for the murderers to come down the road, so he could take his revenge.

Needless to say, when darkness comes, those of the Benton com-munity steer clear of the road beside the old graveyard on U.S. Route 33 where the giant ghost waited—and still may be waiting.

The Haunting of Ruthmere Mansion

I had just begun my telephone conversation with Father George Minnix, the interim director of Ruthmere House Museum, when the alarm system began making its high-pitched screams of warning. Father Minnix's distressed and anxious voice announced, "I must go. The alarm has gone off." Our connection went dead.

Was this yet another in a series of unexplained happenings ru-mored to be plaguing the beautiful Beaux Arts home of the late A.R. Beardsley and his wife?

In the 1880s, Dr. Franklin Miles began marketing his home remedies to Elkhart citizens. Nine years later Albert R. (A.R., as he was known) Beardsley joined the firm. Alfred R. Beardsley's successful life story is the classic American dream. Born in Ohio in 1847, A.R. had completed a common-school education when, as a teenager, he moved to Elkhart to live with his aunt, the widow of his notable uncle Dr. Havilah Beardsley, who established a gristmill. A.R. earned his keep by milking his aunt's cows, doing chores for neighbors, and eventually working as an apprentice clerk in a dry goods store.

In his early twenties, he opened his own dry goods store and became one of the city's leading merchants. Twelve years later he left the dry goods business, purchased stock in the Muzzy Starch Company, and within only six years became the president.

The well-liked and prosperous A.R. soon became part of the political environment at the local level, serving as city clerk, treasurer, and councilman. Finally entering the state arena, he was successful in his bid for Elkhart County's state representative. Continuing to hold state-level positions, he served two terms (1905 and 1907) in the state senate.

Elizabeth Florence Baldwin became his bride in September of 1872. They settled into a house at 307 West High Street. In December 1880, Ruth Beardsley, their first and only child, was born. It soon became apparent, however, that the infant was afflicted with hydrocephalus, a condition in which an abnormal increase of fluid occurs within the cranial cavity. The baby died in July 1881.

After a period of grief, A.R. and Elizabeth began again to entertain friends at their home, something they both loved. As A.R.'s
political popularity grew, though, so did the need for a larger home
in which to host their many friends and political acquaintances.

In 1908 they started building a new home named Ruthmere
along the bank of the Saint Joseph River: Ruth, after their beloved
child, and "mere," meaning "near the water." No expense was
spared in the building of the home, dedicated to the memory of
their child and intended as a warm and welcoming showplace for
their many guests. After two years the Beardsleys moved into their
beautiful new home at 302 East Beardsley. Almost immediately
they began hosting numerous parties, inviting influential friends
and colleagues.

By all accounts (including those of Robert B. Beardsley, the couple's great-nephew,) Elizabeth was quite a lady! Often she'd re-ceive
her guests wearing a hat and gloves and standing in front of the
drawing-room fireplace. Elizabeth was gregarious, hearty, flamboyant, and daring—wearing lipstick and heavy white powder when
few women did so. She was also known for expressing a gentility in
her love of Worth perfume and tea roses, while exhibiting characteristics unbecoming a lady such as swearing when she felt like it,
and later in life, drinking a split of champagne, as prescribed by her
doctor, before going to bed.

The parties ended with the Beardsleys' deaths in 1924 (they
died within five months of each other). Upon their death their
nephew, Arthur Beardsley, purchased the house. He died in 1944,
and the home then passed out of the Beardsley family and was
purchased by a family with five children.

Unfortunately, through the years the property was abandoned and
fell into disrepair. In 1969 the Beardsleys' great-nephew, Robert B.,
began a restoration that took five years to complete. It was opened to
the public in 1973 as a Beaux Arts-style house museum.

During all its years, no "strange" events had ever been reported.
However, today docents and visitors alike have whispered rumors of

experiencing strange and unaccountable happenings. Lights go off and on when no one is in the house. Small items are moved from room to room—a few stories even state that the items have actually been seen "floating." And then there's the mystery of the alarm!

I've been told that frequently the alarm will sound and, upon investigation, nothing is wrong and no one is around. During my telephone conversation with Father Minnix, I heard this phenomena happen.

Later that day I called back and talked to one of the docents. She assured me that she'd never experienced anything out of the ordinary while working in the house. I asked about the alarm that had abruptly ended my telephone conversation earlier that day. She knew that the alarm had sounded, but after investigation by Father Minnix, it was determined nothing was amiss. Although the docent had never heard or experienced anything while working in the house, she did say there was at least one docent who on many occasions had.

Could Ruthmere be haunted? Is it the fun-loving, gregarious, hearty, flamboyant, and daring ghost of Elizabeth?

The Umble Ghost

Goshen College, a college of the Mennonite Church, was founded in 1903. It was a continuation of the Elkhart Institute founded in 1895. In 1920 the college obtained accreditation by the state.

Five years later the arrival of John S. Umble as professor of En-glish marked the beginning of a new era. Among his many accomplishments and achievements for the school were the creation of speech courses and the development of a strong debate program. He believed in the power of communicating. The highly respected and innovative professor died in 1954.

His son, Roy, had joined the faculty in 1946, adding his support and dedication to his father's belief in the power of communications through the establishment of a Drama Department. Although both Umbles taught and stressed the importance of communications, a department dedicated to this discipline was not created until 1972. Within a few years, it became apparent that this department needed a new communications center.

The John S. Umble Center was dedicated in 1978. The inaugural play, Shakespeare's *As You Like It,* was directed by Roy Umble. As more and more students became interested in performing, the Communications Department added a theater major to the curriculum.

As the theater activity picked up in the Umble Center, the students began noticing strange occurrences. In the beginning, little was mentioned, but then the students began talking among themselves, comparing notes. Eventually, the stories became known throughout the campus and gained the attention of English professor and folklore researcher Ervin Beck. During interviews, Beck gathered numerous stories—stories that students believed proved the Umble Center was haunted.

The ghosts manifest themselves through mysterious happenings. Often the ghosts appear to manipulate the electrical switches. Students would turn the lights out as they left rooms, only to discover that they were mysteriously turned back on later. In other instances, if a light was left on in a room, when the student returned, it would be turned off.

Some of the students also reported objects being moved, or even knocked or thrown down. The noise from this activity was frightening and lent credence to the belief that there might be a ghost floating around.

But these weren't the only noises heard by individuals in the building. There were other sounds that, try as they might, those who've heard them could not describe them other than to say, "They're eerie." Many believe that these occurrences are evidence that the ghost of John Umble haunts the Umble Center.

The Weeping Tombstone

November 1903. Most areas were experiencing single-digit tem-
peratures. It was bitterly cold. The ground was frozen. These were
the conditions mourners coped with as they laid Irwin Yoder to rest
in Union Center Cemetery. A young man just twenty-three years
old—his dreams and promises of a happy and prosperous future
ended.

The epitaph chosen was a fond farewell for those who knew
and loved him:

> *Farewell. Dear Friends, From Thee I Am Gone.*
> *My Sufferings Now Are O'er. My Friends Who Knew*
> *and Loved Me Will Know Me Here No More.*

The tombstone bore a photograph of the young man. A transparent cover protected his image from the weather—but not from
vicious vandals. Irwin Yoder's rest was disturbed. His picture was
struck with something hard enough to break the seal. The mystery
of why or who would do such a terrible thing has never been solved.

Sometime after the vandalism, visitors to the site noticed a dark,
tear-shaped stain on Yoder's cheek. An *Elkhart Truth* reporter wrote
in 1984, "If you look closely, you can see the darkening under Yoder's photograph. Some say it's just moisture. But others say the
desecration of his grave marker caused Yoder to weep."

Irwin Yoder's Weeping Tombstone is well known throughout the
community. Many who never knew him now pay him a visit and
wonder: Could it be a tear? A ghostly tear from beyond the grave?

Visit Irwin Yoder in the Union Center Cemetery located at the
intersection of County Road 11 and County Road 50 near Nappanee,
and decide for yourself.

GRANT COUNTY

❖❖❖❖❖❖❖❖❖❖❖THIS COUNTY, HOME of Indiana Wesleyan and Taylor Universities, was founded in 1831 and named for Kentuckians Samuel and Moses Grant, who were killed by Indians in 1789. The same year that the county was founded, the newly platted city of Marion was chosen as the county seat. The city was named for General Francis Marion, a cavalry officer in the Revolutionary War. The county seat was propelled into an industrial boomtown nearly overnight with the discovery of natural gas in 1887.

Marion became known for its iron foundries, paper and glass factories, and manufacturing of auto parts. From 1945 to 1952, Marion made another mark on the automotive industry by manufacturing America's first compact car, the Crosley.

In 1920, The Wesleyan Methodist Church chartered Ma-rion College. Its name was changed to Indiana Wesleyan University in 1988.

Also notorious in Grant County is the annual Easter pa-geant. Each spring since 1937, except during World War II, thousands of local volunteers have presented the pageant in the Marion Coliseum. The production portrays the last week of Christ's life in pantomime and music.

One of the county's most significant locations is a home designed by Frank Lloyd Wright in Marion's residential area, Shady Hills. Its front resembles a tepee. Of historic significance in Grant County is the Miami Indian Cemetery, located on County Route 600-North. The hilltop cemetery was once part of a 6,400-acre Indian Reservation. Since burials were not a part of the Indian traditions, the tombstones at the hilltop cemetery indicate that the Indians buried there were Christians.

Taylor University was originally the Fort Wayne Female College founded by Methodists in 1846. It became Fort Wayne College (co-educational) in 1855. The Upland Land Company offered the school ten thousand dollars and ten acres of land if it would move from Fort Wayne to Grant County. The school accepted the offer and moved to Upland, and in 1890 it was renamed Taylor University in honor of Methodist-Episcopal missionary and bishop, William Taylor.

The town of Matthews was named for Claude Matthews, Indiana governor (1893–1897) and major stockholder in the Matthews Land Company, which founded the town during the natural gas boom. The town seemed to mushroom overnight, hosting numerous industries hoping to profit from the natural gas discovery, and soon became known as the "Wonder City." So enticing was the metropolis that the Indianapolis professional baseball team of the Western Association relocated there in 1901. Matthews's prosperity and growth ended when the gas supply dwindled.

The town of Fairmount, settled primarily by Quakers, was platted in 1850 and originally named Pucker. The name was changed to Fairmount when a citizen visited Philadelphia and returned with glowing reports of the magnificence of Fairmount Park. The town incorporated in 1870.

From 1874 and well into the twentieth century, Fairmont County citizens were successful in their fight against the establishment of saloons in their town. If threats by the vigilantes weren't successful, the dynamiting of saloons usually worked.

Fairmount boosters have made some unsubstantiated claims of greatness for their community, such as, that Fairmount was the home of the Eskimo Pie and the first auto was built by Orlie Scott. On his test drive, Scott wrecked the car, then sold it to Elwood Haynes, who re-stored it, added a brake, and in 1894 made the first successful gas powered "horseless carriage" trial run on Pumpkinvine Pike near Kokomo.

The town has gained national recognition as the home of actor James Dean, who grew up near Fairmount on a farm belonging to his aunt and uncle. In a 1949 state-wide drama contest, he was judged the best actor in Indiana. Soon afterward he left for Hollywood, where he made three pictures before his untimely death in 1955 at the age of twenty-four.

Other notables from Grant County are James Davis, creator of the comic strip Garfield; Thomas R. Marshall, Indiana governor and U.S. Vice President; George W. Steel, Sr., first Oklahoma governor; Kennesaw Mountain Landis, baseball commissioner; Marie Webster, quilt designer and author; Mary Jane Ward, author of *Snake Pit*; Caleb B. Smith, Lincoln's secretary of the interior; and Bishop and Milton Wright, parents of Orville and Wilbur Wright. ❖

Israel Jenkins House

Sara and Randy Ballinger, owners of Marion's Walnut Creek Club Run golf courses, thought they'd heard all the golf stories possible until players at Walnut Creek began telling them of some strange happenings involving a house on their course.

The house, located on the Club Run course at 7453 East 400 South, has been in the Ballinger family since it was first purchased in 1882 from the widow of the original builder, Israel Jenkins. Recently, the Indiana Department of Historic Preservation and Archeology be-stowed upon the house a preservation award that gave it a place on the

Indiana Register of Historic Sites and Structures. Sara and Randy Ballinger have owned the house since 1988. In 2000 they began the restoration to transform the home into an integral part of their golf course.

The original owners, Israel and his wife, Lydia, came to Grant County in 1839. The Jenkinses were one of several Quaker families who were arriving from Clinton County, Ohio. Israel named his two-story brick home "The Elms" for the stately elm trees that lined the drive.

Many Quakers, including two of Jenkins' brothers-in-law, were abolitionists and actively involved in the Underground Railroad. Often homes that were a part of the Underground Railroad system would be given names referring to the type of trees surrounding them to aid slaves in the identification of the houses that offered sanctuary and assistance on the journey to Canada and freedom. It is not known for certain that the Israel Jenkins home was one of these, but it is very possible.

During the 2000 restoration to incorporate the historic home into the Walnut Creek course, workers reported unusual experiences. Some heard footsteps on the stairs, but when they'd go to investigate, there would be no one there. They also experienced some of the other "normal" happenings that occur in most houses that have this type of phenomenon, such as water turning on or off and things being moved. But perhaps one of the strangest occurrences happened to the painter one evening when he was alone in the house.

He often worked alone in the house after dark, but during those nights he began feeling like someone was watching him. On more than one occasion he heard the front door open and close and footsteps on the stairs going to the attic—yet, he was alone! He even reported seeing shadows in the hallway. After these experiences, he would not work in the house alone at night.

It was about three days later when Sara Ballinger described experiencing a similar occurrence. Sara thought she heard the front door open and close and believed it was her husband. Then she heard someone walk up the stairs, down the hall, and up the three steps to the attic door. At that point, it was as if the "person" tried to open the attic door. The latch that kept the door from opening more than about two inches began to rattle.

She didn't realize the painter had also experienced unexplained happenings in the house until later. In both instances, the painter and Sara knew it could not have been a person, because after they heard the sounds, they went to look and no one was there!

Could this ghost be the spirit of the former house owner, Israel Jenkins? Or perhaps of his wife?

Today "The Elms" is a golf club house that serves light refreshments on the first floor. The second floor is used as a museum of historical artifacts of the families and the area.

And still the stories continue. During the summer of 2003, three female members of the golf club described seeing someone looking out the attic window as they finished the eighteenth hole. The women described what appeared to be a young male watching them. Randy assured them that no one was in the attic, but they insisted that they had seen someone watching them from the window.

Randy and the three golfers went upstairs to the attic, where they found the door locked. He unlocked the door, and they entered an empty room. The women showed him where the person had been standing, but there was no indication that any person had been in the room or by the window. It would've been impossible for someone to have unlocked the door and entered the attic room. Randy Ballinger was the only one who had a key, and he had just arrived!

After leaving the attic Randy once again locked the door, and they all went downstairs. He hoped the golfers were somewhat assured no one could've been watching them—at least no one from this world.

Israel Jenkins House on a foggy day.
PHOTO: Jonathan Tétreault

The Phantom of the Opera House

Fairmount, Indiana, is perhaps best known as the hometown of actor James Dean. But there's another stage-struck entity that is making its appearance at the historic Scott Opera House.

In the nineteenth century, many cities and towns were constructing opera houses to bring cultural resources to their citizens. Levi Scott, who was involved in establishing the first Fairmount bank as well as maintaining interest in natural gas resources through the Fairmount Mining Company, undertook the endeavor for Fairmount. In 1884, Scott erected a two-story Italianate building at 116 South Main Street. Scott's opera house was located on the second floor. It was not unusual for opera houses to be built on the second floor since this would allow better utilization of the street level for commercial businesses.

The Fairmount News, in an 1890s account, praised the facility as "one of the nicest and best-arranged to be found in any place this size," adding that "the auditorium had a seating capacity for six hundred people."

The opera house played host to a wide variety of cultural events and persons in its heyday—comedy theater productions, famed Hoosier poet, James Whitcomb Riley, and "silver-tongued" orators addressing such topics as religion, politics, and demon rum.

By the twentieth century, the once-proud building had suffered the ravages of time. It took imagination to see how the building could have been such a focus of cultural life and entertainment for the town. The stage and seats were removed, and a partition had been built dividing the space into two rooms.

In 1993 came new signs of hope that the Scott Opera House may once again be a focal point of community cultural activity. A group of local residents interested in preserving Fairmount's architectural and cultural heritage began meeting and studying the possibility of community revitalization. From the beginning, the primary goal was the restoration of the Scott Opera House for use as both a community arts and cultural center.

During this time, students began using the old opera house for band rehearsals. It wasn't long before strange things began to happen.

Judy Cowling, president of Historic Fairmount, first heard the ghost stories from her son, Andy, the band's guitarist. The students had been so spooked by their experiences that they were convinced there was a real phantom in the opera house.

One evening, Andy placed a coil of guitar wire on one of the speakers. A few minutes later he watched as the coil mysteriously unwound and began rising into the air like someone was stretching it.

Cowling tried to explain away the various reports that began coming from the band members. The eerie noises? That's typical of old buildings. The lights going off and on with no one around? The electrical system needed to be checked or there could be a short in the wiring. And when band members reported that objects they'd put down would be moved to other locations, Cowling said it was probably one of the boys playing tricks on the others.

Then one night a band member saw a disembodied face of a bearded man! Cowling had no explanation, and the kids were really frightened. They began carrying Bibles to rehearsals.

Still Cowling was skeptical. She wasn't convinced there was anything supernatural about the "unexplained" happenings. To prove this to the kids and alleviate their anxieties, she decided to spend an evening in the old opera house with the band.

At one point that evening, Judy Cowling opened the unlocked door of one of the building's rooms, entered, and shut the door behind her. When she tried to reopen the door, she discovered it was locked! Eventually, she was able to force the door open.

Could this be the proof she needed that the building had a phantom? She shrugged off the incident, instead choosing to believe that the old door must have gotten stuck.

The mystery is still a mystery. It's still possible there's a phantom in the old Opera House.

The Spirit of Hostess House

A few years ago, a very sad and unfortunate event occurred at the Wilson-Vaughan house, located at 723 West Fourth Street in Marion—today known as the Hostess House. An elderly house-keeper tragically died there. The circumstances of the woman's death are well known. Her loss to the community, friends, and family is still very painful. As so often happens in such circumstances, stories began circulating that a ghost had been seen in one of the upstairs windows. Those who say they've seen this apparition be-lieve it to be that of the elderly housekeeper. There could be another explanation, however: It could be Lillian "Peggy" Wilson, the wo-man the house had been built for as a wedding present.

Far more intriguing than any of its residents may be the spirit of the Hostess House itself. The house's tale of love, rejection, and remorse has endured half a century and no doubt will continue for many generations to come.

The historical Hostess House, rumored to a tragic presence.
PHOTO: Peggy McClelland

The historically significant house is considered to be one of Grant County's treasures. J. Woodrow Wilson, a prominent Marion bank-er, built the twenty-four room mansion as a wedding present for his wife, Lillian "Peggy" Pamell Wilson. Sadly, the newlyweds only lived in the house a short time, when Peggy, at age twenty-nine, became a widow in 1916.

After her husband's death the young, wealthy, and vivacious widow traveled in the sophisticated circles of New York and Chicago. Noted to be a delightful hostess, she often entertained her rich and famous New York and Chicago friends at her beautiful home in Marion.

While attending a party in Chicago in 1919, she was introduced to the famous poet and author of the *Spoon River Anthology,* Edgar Lee Masters. He was fifty-one years old. She was thirty-two. Masters, though married, was well known for becoming involved with rich, sophisticated women. Peggy seemed drawn to men of prominence and artistic success. It wasn't long before their meeting turned into a love affair.

Masters made several visits to Indiana to visit Peggy at her mansion. They also met in Paris, London, and at Masters's retreat in Michigan. The affair lasted about two years.

In 1921 Masters attempted to obtain a divorce from his wife so that he could marry Peggy. Before the year's end, though, Peggy's ardor had drastically cooled. Masters learned that the great love of his life had been seeing other men and indeed, in 1926, she married Dr. John C. Vaughan.

The romance and his life shattered, the embittered Masters "told all" in his book *Mirage,* published in 1924. Many of Peggy's Marion friends knew of Masters's visits to the mansion, but they were unaware of the love affair between the famous poet and the prominent widow until this book came out.

Peggy continued to entertain and travel between Marion and New York, where she died in 1952. Masters and his wife were divorced. He remarried and moved to New York. Ironically, the two ex-lovers, whose romance would live on forever in the pages of

American literature, apparently never knew they lived only a short distance apart in their later years.

Has the spirit of Peggy been seen in an upstairs window? Is she remorseful and waiting for Edgar Lee Masters? Or could she simply be waiting to once more entertain the many famous and rich who were a part of her world? Her presence is certainly felt in this elegant and beautiful home.

Perhaps the answer to the question whether Peggy, in spirit, re-mains within in the Hostess House can be found in the last lines of Masters's 1926 poem titled "Peggy."

"It's night now, Peggy, and the electric arc
Throws lavender lights upon your brow;
You are a ghost now, and I bow
Myself into the dark."

The Ghost of Mason's Bridge

It happened one cold fall night, near midnight, under the full moon: The sounds of angry voices, then blood-curdling screams, and finally the splashing sound of something falling or being thrown into the river below the bridge.

Sometime during the early 1940s, a husband and wife began an argument that resulted in both of their deaths. The house where they lived is said to have been on a hill just outside of Gas City about five hundred feet from the road near Mason's Bridge.

The argument began when the husband accused his wife of having an affair. His jealous rage became maniacal. Fearing for her life, his wife fled from the house, her husband close behind her brandishing an ax.

He caught up with his wife just as she reached Mason's Bridge. With ferocity, he swung the ax and cut off her head. Picking it up, he tossed her head over the bridge and into the water below. Ex-hausted, he sat on the roadway beside his wife's headless body.

Maybe it was the chill of the night—or the chill in his heart—that shocked him back into a semblance of sanity and the realization of the horror that he had committed.

Overcome with grief and guilt, he returned to the house, climbed onto the roof, and hung himself.

That's how it happened then—and how it still happens—or so the legend goes.

To witness the reoccurring murder at Mason's Bridge, go there around midnight on a clear fall night with a full moon. Take State Route 22 out of Gas City to County Road 500 East. Park your car and walk to the east side of the bridge. Wait, watch, and listen.

Soon you will hear voices raised in anger, arguing, and the sound of people running down the hill toward the bridge. As the sounds reach the bridge two images begin to take shape. One small. One large. The larger of the two raises something above its head. The moonlight glints off the object. Suddenly a sickening dull thud is heard, mingled with a spine-chilling scream, and then—silence.

Wait a bit before you move—if you can move. Then go to the opposite side of the bridge and look along the river's bank. There you will see a white figure walking along the edge of the river—the woman looking for her head.

Mason's Bridge and the haunted river banks below. PHOTO: Peggy McClelland

JASPER COUNTY

❖❖❖❖❖❖❖❖❖ JASPER COUNTY WAS formed in 1835, organized in 1838, and named for Sgt. William Jasper of South Carolina, a Revolutionary War hero. Most of the county's central and northern portions were water-logged, especially in the famous Kankakee swamp. The Kankakee was ten miles wide and covered nearly 500,000 acres, making it one of the largest swamps in the United States.

Illinois land speculator Benjamin J. Gifford purchased approximately 35,000 acres at $4.50 an acre. He ditched and drained the area, turning the land into productive tenant farms yielding corn, oats, onions, and potatoes. He even built his own thirty-two-mile railroad—the Chicago and Wabash Valley, popularly known as the "Onion Belt"—to carry his crops and livestock to the Illinois market.

In the 1890s one of Gifford's tenant farmers was digging a well and struck oil. Eventually, there were more than one hundred active wells on Gifford's farms, producing four hundred barrels per day.

Shortly thereafter the town of Asphaltum was founded, and a refinery and several oil well equipment manufacturers located there. The boom and the industries ended quickly, but fifty years later, farmers continued to grease machinery with the heavy petroleum that still oozed from the ground.

New York merchant James Van Rensselaer arrived in Jasper County in 1838 and built a gristmill. The following year he platted a town and named it Newton for Sir Isaac Newton. In 1841 the name was changed to Rensselaer, which became Jasper's county seat and eventually the largest city in the area.

James F. Hanley (1892–1942) was Rensselaer's most fa-mous son. A prodigious composer, he provided many songs for movies and stage plays. His song "Indiana" (better known as "Back Home Again in Indiana") is the recognized anthem at the Indianapolis Motor Speedway's 500.

The village of Collegeville was founded in 1889 and named for Saint Joseph's College, which was incorporated the same year. The Catholic Church-supported school be-came a four-year liberal arts college in 1936, and until 1968 it remained all male. The National Football League's Chicago Bears used the campus as their preseason training camp from 1944 to 1974. ❖

Moody Road Lights

Most Jasper and Pulaski County residents have heard one or more of the many stories concerning the mystery of the Moody Road lights. The stories connected with these lights have extended far beyond the two counties. The lights have even been featured on the television show *Unsolved Mysteries*.

You must first go to the location on Moody Road to experience the creepy phenomena. Go after dark and preferably on a moonless night. From Francesville in Pulaski County, take County Road 500 South until you enter Jasper County, where the road becomes County Road 200 South. Continue until it intersects with County Road 230 East. At that point, Moody Road is a short distance north. Follow Moody Road until you come to Meridian Road.

From Rensselaer, drive east on State Route 114 to County Road 400 West and turn north. Continue until it intersects with County Road 400 South. At that point, turn east, continuing on until you reach County Road 20 East. Turning north, you will travel a short distance to Moody Road. Turning west, you will reach Meridian Road, and the location of the Moody lights.

Be certain your car is facing north. Turn off your engine, blink your lights three times, and then turn them off. Now, sitting in the dark, prepare yourself for a visit from the mysterious Moody Road lights. They will come. First you'll see an orb-shaped orange light. It seems to go away and then reappear several times. The light will change from orange to red and from large to small. And you may see as many as four lights bobbing in the night. Intrepid individuals already taking this journey have stated that the orbs darted toward their cars, then quickly retreated, or even crossed the road and back again.

Some explain these "mysterious" lights as just headlights from cars on Highway 49, which is approximately two miles north of Meridian road. Others believe that since this is a low-lying area, the phenomenon is created by swamp gas.

A more supernatural story surrounding the Moody Road lights goes back to horse-and-buggy days. Two brothers were "joy riding" in the family buggy. It was a dark and moonless night. One of the wagon wheels hit a rock on the road, and one of the brothers fell off. Before the other brother could stop the racing horses, the fallen brother had been decapitated by the buggy's rear wheels. His head was never found. Every night after his chores were completed, his remorseful brother went out with a lantern looking for his brother's head.

According to legend, along Moody Road where the corn grows high, you can still see the brother's lantern. The light passes one row at a time. It glows orange as he passes through the field, and becomes red when he reaches the end of a row. The light then turns and moves through another row of corn. You can see the light glowing above the corn stalks. It slowly moves to the end and back, moving up a row, down a row, closer and closer—one row at a time. What happens if the phantom and his light reach your car is not known. No one has stayed long enough to find out.

Another story associated with the lights concerns the Mafia. A contract had been issued on the life of a man. His name is not known, nor is his connection with the crime organization. According to the story, he and his teenage daughter were hiding out in an old farm house on Moody Road. During their stay, she had made friends with some youths in the area. It was her birthday, and she wanted to go out and have fun with her new friends. Her father was against her going, but he could deny her nothing and agreed with one very important stipulation: When they brought her home, they must not bring her to the house. They should stop near Meridian Road, flash their lights three times, and wait. He would come and get her. That way he would know that it was not the Mafia coming to kill him.

Today, if you go to this road, flash your lights three times, and wait, some say you will see the outline of a man walking with a lantern swinging back and forth, the light changing from orange to red to yellow, then veering off into the cornfield. Many believe it is the girl's father. But what happened that night? Why does her father haunt Moody Road waiting for the signal from his daughter?

In this same vicinity on Moody Road is a cemetery. The oldest known burial dates 1849, with burials continuing into the mid-twentieth century. This location has given rise to another explanation to the mysterious lights: a haunting love story.

Two lovers were walking hand in hand down the road, oblivious of anything but their love. Suddenly the sound of gunfire broke the silence of the night. The man fell beside the road. The girl ran across the road and into the cemetery, hoping to find safety behind a monument. She, too, was shot and killed.

The criminal was never found, nor was a reason for this heinous crime. Could she have been the teenage daughter walking with her boyfriend and waiting for her father? Were they killed by a Mafia hit man? Is this why the father still haunts the road looking for his daughter? Or, are these legends two separate Moody Road tragedies?

Many have parked at midnight near the cemetery, watched, and waited, hoping to catch a glimpse of the woman's ghost leaving the cemetery and crossing the road to the cornfield where her lover had died.

A resident of the area, George Johnson, says he has heard all the stories. He included some of them in his book, *Indian and Nature Stories,* which is a two-year collection of his weekly local newspaper column, "By George."

His own theory of the Moody Road Lights is based on distant headlights that create ghost-like images in the fog. The intersection of Meridian and Moody Road is located on a high glacial moraine ridge. This high point overlooks a low-lying muck swamp ground. About two miles north of this junction is Indiana State Highway 49, which runs perpendicular into Indiana 14. After dark, when vehicles travel down Indiana 49, their headlights bounce up and down and are reflected on the low ground fog. When they turn either east or west at Indiana 14, it makes the "ghost lights" move and disappear. Perhaps this is logical, but that may be the problem with his theory. Where ghosts are involved, the only logical explanation is the simple belief that they exist.

LAGRANGE COUNTY

❖❖❖❖❖❖❖❖❖ THE COUNTY was organized in 1832 and named for Marquis de Lafayette's country home near Paris. The county seat, Lagrange, was platted in 1836.

Lagrange County is home to the Pigeon River State Fish and Wildlife Area headquarters, just east of the town of Mongo. Created in the 1950s, the 11,500-acre state facility contains marshes, hydraulic dams, and a one-hundred-acre nature preserve featuring the largest tamarack bog forest in Indiana. The facility also offers state-regulated fishing and hunting, camping, canoeing, picnicking, bird watching, and mushroom and berry picking.

A large Amish population now inhabits Lagrange County, and Shipshewana is a bustling center for buying and selling Amish goods. The town was founded in 1889 and named after Chief Shipshewana, leader of the Potawatomi Indians who lived in the area. ❖

She Still Waits

Lagrange County, founded in 1832, was still sparsely inhabited when a young couple from New York settled on land somewhere between Howe and Cedar Lake. They built a sturdy three-story home out of bricks delivered from Fort Wayne. The home featured a tall, castle-like turret towering above its roof.

The couple lived in tranquility until the Civil War erupted. Perhaps hoping they were too far removed from the war, they stayed to themselves. But one day, the husband was called to duty as an officer in the Union Army. They were childless, and when the husband left, the young wife found herself alone and isolated. It is said she spent most of her days in the turret, watching the countryside, and hoping to see her husband on his horse riding home to her.

Day after day, she watched. Unwilling to cease her vigil even when night came, she began sitting in the turret with a lamp lit hoping to see her husband, illuminated by the moon, riding toward home. Finally her worst fear came true on that fateful day when she received word that he had been killed. She now felt totally alone and forsaken. She retreated further into herself and her home, never venturing out, grieving herself into insanity and death.

The house stayed vacant for years, but before it disappeared from the landscape, people in the area said that at night, if the wind was just right, they could hear the woman moaning, and crying out her husband's name. Some people even professed to see a light in the turret window.

Of course, this is only a story people tell—especially around Halloween. Or is it?

LAKE COUNTY

❖❖❖❖❖❖❖❖❖ THIS COUNTY was organized in 1837 and named for Lake Michigan, which is the county's northern border. The first county seat, a settlement founded by George Earle, was established at Liverpool in 1839. A year later the county seat was transferred to Crown Point, which was originally called Robinson's Prairie, for Solon and Milo Robinson. A legend surrounds the name change. When Solon Robinson saved his neighbors' lands from speculators, he was nicknamed "King of the Squatters"; hence, the settlement became known as Crown Point: "Crown" for the "king," and "Point" for the elevation on which the courthouse and Robinson's cabin stood.

The old Lake County Courthouse, known as "The Grand Old Lady," was erected in 1878. After the county government agencies moved to new facilities in the 1970s, a nonprofit organization formed to restore the Georgian and Romanesque-style building. Today it houses a restaurant, shops, and the Lake County Historical Society.

In 1909 the Cobe Cup Race, the first major auto race in the United States, was held just south of the Court House on a twenty-five-mile track. The winner was Louis Chevrolet, a Swiss-born mechanic who would later go on to found the Chevrolet Motor Company.

From 1915–1940 Crown Point was known as the "marriage mill." Marriages without waiting were performed around the clock, seven days a week. It is believed that more than 175,000 couples were married during this period. Some of the more famous ceremonies involved Rudolph Valentino, Ronald Reagan (and Jane Wyman), Tom Mix, Red Grange, Muhammed Ali, and Joe DiMaggio.

Crown Point was also famous for notorious bank robber John Dillinger's renowned 1934 jail break.

In the 1890s, the community of Cedar Lake was established as a resort town on the Lake of the Red Cedars, named for the red cedars that grew in abundance along its shore. During the 1920s, Chicago gangsters, tourists, and prominent persons flocked to the resort town. Its heyday ended with the 1929 depression.

For many years Murrell Belanger operated a farm-implement store in the town of Lowell. On the second floor of his building, located on Mill Street, he built racecars from 1945–1966. His famous No. 99 won the Indianapolis 500 race in 1951, at an average speed of 126.244 miles per hour. In 1976 the building was destroyed in a fire.

Hammond was settled in 1851 and platted in 1875 by M.M. Towle. Along with his five brothers, Towle operated a hotel, meat market, packing house, and publishing company. Originally the settlement was called Hohman, for Ernest Hohman, an early settler. Later it was called State Line for its location on the Indiana-Illinois line. Finally, it was renamed for George H. Hammond, a Detroit butcher who founded the local slaughterhouse and adapted the refrigerated boxcar for shipping dressed beef.

Hoosier author Jean Shepherd spent his formative years in Hammond where he attended Harding Elementary School and graduated from Hammond High School in 1939. The house he lived in during the 1920s and 1930s is located at 2907 Cleveland Street. Shepherd uses the city's former name, Hohman, as the setting of his humorous novel *In God We Trust, All Others Pay Cash*. ❖

The Ghosts of Cline Avenue

Many Mexican immigrants moved to the Lake County region in the 1940s because of the area's thriving steel industry. They brought with them the Mexican folk tale of La Llorona.

When a ghost in a blood-stained white dress began haunting the intersection of Cline Avenue and Fifth Avenue in the predominately Mexican neighborhood, the spirit was referred to as La Llorona.

La Llorona is an ancient Mexican legend. The story goes that a wealthy man's son fell in love with a young woman from a poor family. They had two children by this illicit union. She dreamed and longed for the day when he would marry her. This would ensure that her children would not have to live in poverty.

Finally she asked the man when they would marry. He laughed at her saying that this would never be. She was hurt and confused. Returning to the humble home she shared with their children, she decided the children would be better off dead. In that moment of desperation and madness, she got a knife and murdered them.

Her white dress stained with blood, she went to the man's home and informed him that she'd killed their children. The man had her thrown out and told her never to come back. Throughout the next few weeks, she was seen at night walking all over town still wearing the blood-stained dress. Insane and in denial of what she had done, she searched for her children.

The police were eventually informed of the crime, but before they could arrest her, she was found dead in a nearby river. It is said that her spirit still wanders the streets in a blood-stained dress, looking for her children.

Besides this Mexican legend, however, there have been many other haunting tales along the length of Cline Avenue, which begins in Gary and ends just before the Illinois border. Indications are that there are more than one spirit dressed in white.

Sightings by motorists on Cline Avenue have described a woman standing by the side of the road late at night in a white blood-stained dress. Those who have stopped to offer assistance found she had disappeared into the night. Others have reported that she made wild motions with her hands, and screamed something about her children, and then disappeared into the night. Who is this Cline Avenue spirit?

One of the stories told is that of a woman driving between Gary and Hammond with her young children. She missed a turn, lost control, and swerved off the road. She was thrown clear of the car, but her children were killed in the accident. The mother's grief was so deep she lost touch with reality, returning to the scene time and again searching for her children. She continued her search until her death—and those who have seen the Cline Avenue ghost say she's still searching.

Another story begins with the seventeen-year-old daughter of Polish immigrants. Her name was Sophia. By all accounts she was a beautiful young woman with long blonde hair and bright blue eyes. Her parents hoped she would find a nice young Polish man, settle down, and have a family. Many eligible young men courted her, but none of them had a chance of capturing Sophia's heart.

Unknown to anyone, she had already fallen in love with a man six years older and from another ethnic group. From the beginning Sophia and her beloved recognized that their parents would never accept their love. They secretly met on the banks of the Calumet River near the outskirts of Hammond, where they shared their dreams that someday they could be together forever.

They decided to elope and be married by a priest in Griffith. On that day Sophia told her parents she would be working late and afterward would be spending the night with a friend. She left her parents' home for the last time and made her way to a dress shop, where she purchased her wedding dress. She then took a cab to the church in Griffith.

She waited at the church for two hours, but the groom never came. Distraught, she ran from the church. Still wearing her wedding dress, she hailed a cab to take her back to Hammond. As they passed the Calumet River, she asked the driver to stop. Getting out of the cab, she ran into the river and disappeared. The driver raced to the police station to report the incident. Two days later a fisherman found her body.

It is said that her spirit still haunts Cline Avenue. Cars passing by often report seeing a beautiful woman in what is described as a wedding dress. As they watch in amazement, the woman runs toward the river and disappears.

A cab driver on his way to Hammond reported a different experience with perhaps this same ghost. He was stopped by a young lady with long blonde hair, and was puzzled by the fact that she appeared to be wearing a wedding gown. As he pulled back into traffic, he asked where she wanted to be taken. Glancing in his rearview mirror when he received no answer, he nearly wrecked his cab. There was no one in the backseat!

Is there more than one lady in white haunting Cline Avenue? Or, are these just different versions of the same ghost story? Either way, few question or doubt that there is a female ghost dressed in white haunting Cline Avenue—far too many have seen her.

He's Still in the Game

In 1848 Michael and Judith Johnston were the first settlers in what would become the village of Highland. Growth was slow until the establishment of a railroad station in 1882. By 1910, when Highland was incorporated, the population had increased to three hundred. When the twenty-first century arrived, the village population had reached nearly 24,000.

Highland, located in the northwest corner of Indiana, is considered a suburb of Chicago. The school system is known regionally and throughout the state of Indiana for its excellence in education. The system consists of four elementary schools, a middle school, and the high school at 913 South Erie Street. The combined student enrollment is approximately 3,270 students—plus one ghost.

For several years students have been telling stories about the haunting of the Highland High School gym. When entering the facility, people have reported seeing a boy roaming aimlessly around. Sometimes they've watched him running laps around the basketball court. Often when students and teachers enter the gym, they're greeted by the sounds of a basketball being bounced. And yet, there isn't anyone there.

Nobody is afraid of the young ghost. He's only doing what the other boys do—running warm-up laps and taking hoop shots. But who is he and what is his story?

Students believe this spirit to be the ghost of Bob Haymaker. Bob died one day in gym class while playing basketball. He had collapsed on the floor, and his teammates and teacher helped him to the bench where he seemed to recover. His teacher pronounced that he was fine. The next time the teacher looked over at the bench, however, Bob Haymaker was lying on the floor—dead.

Ever since then, Bob Haymaker has haunted the Highland High School gym, perhaps waiting to be called into the game once again.

Restless Spirits

Cemeteries provide many tales of hauntings. Why are there so many reported sightings in cemeteries? Perhaps it's just the nature of the place. Frequently it appears some of the dearly departed like to kick up their heels a bit.

In Lake County, several cemeteries are believed to be haunted. One of these is Southeast Grove Cemetery near Lowell, also known as the Gypsies' Graveyard. Its graves date back to the early 1800s, and that is where the legend begins.

A band of Gypsies set up camp in the area. At that time, Gypsies were believed to have powers beyond the comprehension of ordinary folks. Tales of pagan rituals circulated and farmers began reporting disappearances of their livestock. The Gypsies were warned by a delegation from the community that they should leave.

An influenza epidemic hit the Gypsy campsite. The townspeople refused to help or provide medicine. Many of the Gypsies died and were buried near the campsite. Those who survived left the area, but not before they laid a curse on the townspeople and their descendants, proclaiming that their Gypsy dead would haunt the area forever. The site where they'd buried their dead is what later became the Southeast Grove Cemetery—or the Gypsies' Graveyard.

Today, there are those who believe the tale and others who state emphatically, "There ain't no Gypsy graveyard around here."

What is the explanation then for what has been seen and experienced by those who've visited the cemetery? With gravesites dating back to the early 1800s, you'd expect the earth over the graves to be like the rest of the ground. This is not true in the Gypsies' Graveyard. According to legend, visitors have reported finding fresh dirt in the older graves as if they had just been filled in! Some brave individuals have dared to venture to the area at night. They've returned with stories about being greeted by a party of glowing figures ad-vancing toward them. None of those visitors stayed to accept the hospitality of the Gypsies' Graveyard residents, however.

Lake Prairie Cemetery is another location with a reputation for strange and unexplained activities. Those who are familiar with this cemetery agree that most of the activity is confined to the southern half, the location of the earliest burials. Rising mists have been seen floating across the grounds in what could be described as a ghostly waltz. Sightings of orbs—glowing balls of light that torment the imagination of the observer—have also been reported. Are they just spots before the observer's eyes? Imagination? Or spirit energies released from those buried in the old section?

Griffith also has a very spooky story about a burial site called Ross Cemetery. According to legend, during a terrific thunderstorm in the 1950s, a teenage couple was driving on the road that passed the cemetery on their way home from the high school prom. No one knows what happened, but the car crashed. They were both found dead. The girl, named Elizabeth, had been thrown a few feet from the car, and her boyfriend had been pinned behind the steering wheel.

Since the accident there have been numerous reports of a young girl hitchhiking along the road. One such sighting came twenty years after the accident when a high school boy was driving home after football practice. Deciding to take a short cut, he turned on the road that passed by Ross Cemetery. He was surprised to see a teenage girl in a party dress standing on the side of the road. He stopped and offered her a ride. Thinking she must be cold wearing only a prom dress, he offered her his letter jacket, which she accepted while climbing into the back seat. When he inquired as to where she was going she gave him directions to what he believed was her home. As they approached Ross Cemetery she asked him to stop. Wondering why she wanted him to stop at the cemetery, he turned to ask and discovered she was gone—along with his jacket.

Assuming she had somehow jumped out of the car before he realized it and was somewhere in the cemetery, he began looking for her. He found his jacket draped across a tombstone marking the gravesite of a girl whose first name was Elizabeth.

The road passing this cemetery has since been closed. Some believe it's because of the ghostly hitchhiker.

MIAMI COUNTY

❖❖❖❖❖❖❖❖❖THE COUNTY was organized in 1834 and named for the big miami reserve, on which the county was established, and for the Miami Indian nation. Peru was laid out as the county seat in 1834. Many early settlers came from Peru, New York, which was believed to be named after the South American country. Peru is also said to be a Miami word meaning "a straight place in the river."

A post office named McGregor, the first postmaster's name, was established in the Peru area in January 1829. The name was changed in March that year to Miamisport and later to Peru.

Four miles east of Peru just off State Route 124 is the Godfroy Cemetery, a Miami burial ground formerly called Massasinaway. Only American Indians and their white spouses were allowed to be buried here. The last Miami war chief, Francis Godfroy, the son of a French trader and a Miami mother, and his descendants are buried here.

Benjamin Wallace, a Peru livery stable owner, acquired several small circuses in 1884, which he merged to create one. The circus eventually traveled under the name of the Great Wallace Show. In 1891, he purchased five hundred acres just outside of Peru from Chief Godfroy, and the land became the winter headquarters for the circus. Soon other circuses, such as the Clyde-Beatty Cole Brothers shows, Sells-Floto, and Buffalo Bill's Wild West Show, moved their winter quarters to the Peru area. In the 1920s Peru became known as the "Circus City." The site of the old winter quarters is now the home of the International Circus Hall of Fame.

Located on North Broadway is the Circus City Center

and Museum. The museum contains memorabilia from circuses that made Peru their home, including posters, costumes, a wild animal cage, and furniture from the Wallace circus train. The center conducts a circus school for children, many of whom are descendants of circus stars. Since 1960 Peru has revived its circus tradition in the annual weeklong Circus City Festival held the third Wednesday in July. Most performers are children from the circus school.

Composer Cole Porter (1891–1964) was born in Peru at 102 East Third Street. The well-known composer wrote more than thirty musical comedies, including *Kiss me Kate* (1948) and *Can Can* (1953). He was the son of a Peru druggist and the grandson of one of the richest men in the nation. Porter's grandfather, James Omar, made millions of dollars prospecting for gold in California and speculating in West Virginia timber and coal. ❖

On the Banks of the Wabash

In 1927, the town of Peru was shocked by what was discovered in the depths of a working gravel pit about two hundred feet south of the banks of the Wabash. While gathering gravel, workers came upon an unexpected and grisly sight: a human skeleton. The skeleton, found just about two feet below the surface, was in a sitting position with the head bent resting on its knees, as if the individual had become weary, sat down to rest, and fell asleep.

There was nothing else found in the grave. Not a scrap of clothing, not a piece of jewelry, nothing else was found to aid in the identification of the individual. The skeleton was removed to the morgue where it was determined that the deceased was a man, past his middle years, who had been there for some time.

When word got out about the gruesome find, it was hoped that older citizens might remember a story told during their youth that could help solve the mystery. No one came forward with a possible solution, nor did a search through historical records uncover information concerning a pioneer cemetery. Finally the authorities closed the case with the determination that the remains were from the early Wabash River days, probably that of a French trader or trapper.

The gravel pit, across from the current West City Park, has since been filled in, and a home has been built on the site.

According to Miami County Museum Archivist Nancy Masten, the mysterious remains were given to the museum and are still there. In the nineties they were loaned to Ball State University for examination to determine their age, origin, and cause of death, and then they were returned. Even with this examination, no one is completely certain of the identity. The early records and Ball State's findings are not in agreement.

Sometime after the discovery of the remains, citizens near the area reported seeing strange lights floating just above the ground near the gravel pit. There were several possible explanations for this phenomenon—clouds of lightning bugs, a phosphorescence due to decaying vegetation, reflections, or more likely, imagination. Soon there were reports of other strange happenings at the site: mournful sounds floating on the night air accompanied by opaque mists creeping about the trees and hovering along the bank.

When the skeleton was dug up, had the man's soul been released from its long-hidden grave? Are the mysterious orbs and mists apparitions of the tortured soul of a man who had been murdered? Rumors began circulating that the spirit of the man was lurking on the banks of the Wabash, seeking justice and revenge on those who had killed him.

NEWTON COUNTY

❖❖❖❖❖❖❖❖❖❖ FOUNDED IN 1859 and named for Sgt. John Newton, who served under Francis Marion in the Revolutionary War, Newton County was the last Indiana county to be organized.

Kentland is the county seat. The town was platted in August 1860 by Alexander Kent and originally named Kent. Two months later, the name was changed to Kent Station, and four years later the name was changed again to Adriance. Finally, in 1868, it was changed to its current name of Kentland.

The town of Morocco was established in 1851 and apparently named after the country in North Africa. There is a legend stating that the town was given the name Morocco for a pair of boots that were topped with red morocco leather. The small community was the home of Edgar (Sam) Rice, an American League outfielder and one of the few Hoosiers elected to the national Baseball Hall of Fame. Rice played from 1915 to 1934, had a lifetime batting average of .322, and set defensive records.

Morocco was also the home of John Ade, father of author George Ade. When he was twelve years old John's family moved to America and settled near Cincinnati. John married Adaline Bush of Ohio in 1851, and two years later they settled in Morocco. In 1860 the first county election was held, and John Ade became Newton County's first recorder. At that time, the family moved to the county seat of Kentland.

Just outside of the tiny town of Brook is Hazelden, the home of author George Ade (1866–1944). A Kentland native, he's best known as a playwright, humorist, author, and newspaper columnist. In the 1900s he was the first

author to have three Broadway plays running simultane-
ously. Playwright Neil Simon has since matched this
accomplishment. Ade's English Manor/Tudor-style house,
where he lived alone as a bachelor, was built in 1904 at
the cost of $25,000. Hazelden quickly became a nation-
ally known social and political gathering place. William
Howard Taft opened his successful bid for the presidency
at Hazelden in 1908, and President Theodore Roosevelt
was a frequent guest of Ade's. ❖

Kentland Area Hauntings

Newton was the last of Indiana's ninety-two counties to be established. The county seat, Kentland, is just two miles north of the
Benton County line and approximately seven miles west of the
Illinois state line. The county is perhaps best known as the home
of the internationally famous humorist and author George Ade,
whose residence is now an Historic Landmark.

Others are also well known to the citizens of Kentland and
Sheldon, Illinois. Many of them can be found in Illinois just over
the state line. They've never written a book, been on television, or
appeared in the movies. For the most part, they do not seek out
attention. But from time to time, they do appear. For generations
their stories have been known and told in the surrounding areas.
Some are known to roam in three locations not far from Kentland:
the Crescent City Bridge, Iroquois Trestle, and Lantern's Lane.
Another lingers in a cemetery, and another, a farm.

The best time to meet these elusive, legendary individuals is at
nightfall. Starting from Kentland, follow U.S. Route 24 west to Crescent City, Illinois—a short drive of approximately twenty miles. Continue west until you come to Route 49. Then turn north, following
Route 49 to road 1900 North. Follow that road a short distance until
you see an iron truss bridge. You will arrive at the first meeting site.

There's a sad and haunting story about this bridge. One night some teenagers were walking on the bridge when a car approached. The driver was either speeding or didn't see them. There wasn't time to get out of the way. The car plowed into the small group. All died there on the bridge.

Those who have stopped their cars on this bridge in the dark swear they've heard tapping on the car door, and some have even seen a face peering through the passenger-side window. Others report seeing the figure of a man appear. The apparition seems to be composed of wavy lines like shimmering heat waves.

Other phenomena reported are glowing orbs. Some people even say that as they leave the bridge and look in the rearview mirror, the bridge seems to glow red.

Another Illinois site, the Iroquois Trestle, is just forty miles out of Kentland. Begin your journey on u.s. Route 24—or you could call it "the ghost road"—to Sheldon, Illinois. Out of Sheldon take u.s. Route 52 to the town of Iroquois and County Road 2880 East. Keep on the lookout for County Road 2000 North. Follow this road until it forks, then go to the right. Soon you'll see the railroad trestle.

Nearly two decades ago at this spot, a train derailment killed an engineer. Since that time, visitors to the trestle have reported strange sounds and a sense of foreboding—or even sheer terror. Balls of light dip and sway and dance along the tracks. Often they begin to move toward the observers, causing them to turn and run away. Could the lights be the dead engineer's lantern? Is he still out there trying to determine what caused the derailment and his death?

Some people have heard the sound of footsteps walking the tracks. Again, could it be the engineer? Others have reported sounds in the water like someone treading, trying to keep from drowning.

On at least one occasion, a curious visitor had an entirely different experience. As he stood near the trestle, he heard strange rustlings in the woods behind him. Something was coming closer and closer. He quickly got in his car and left, never to return again. Could there be more than one ghost at this site?

On this ghostly Kentland-area tour, the next visit is the country road south of Woodland, Illinois, known as Lantern's Lane. Here you will meet a man and his wife who have been walking this lane for more than two hundred years.

Their tale begins on a day in the 1800s. The husband went into town and planned to return late that evening. His waiting wife became worried as darkness fell across the fields. The sounds of night filled the air and still she did not hear the horse's hooves approach.

Concerned that something had happened to him along the roadway, she lit a lantern and went out to search for him. No one knows if she ever found him. After that night, the two were never seen again—at least not in their corporeal form. Through the years many have encountered the ethereal couple walking the road, now known far and wide as Lantern's Lane.

Once you arrive at Lantern's Lane, park your car in the middle of the road, turn the lights and engine off, and wait. Soon you will hear it: the sound of a horse's hooves as the unseen horse and his rider pass you by. Then, as your eyes adjust to the darkness, you'll begin to see an amber light in the distance. At first it's unclear as to what you're seeing, but soon you'll realize it is a light from a lantern coming closer and closer. Did the wife and husband meet up on this road, or are they still on their separate spectral paths?

At one point, Lantern's Lane also had a haunted house that was rumored to be the home of the vanished couple. Recently it was demolished, but before its "demise," thrill-seekers made frequent visits and told chilling stories of their experiences.

In one story, a group entered the house and decided to first in-vestigate the basement. As they attempted to descend into the depths of the cellar, something they could only describe as an "in-visible force" held them back. Frightened, they made their way back up the stairs and out the door. One of the girls in the group saw what she took to be a sewing pattern on the floor, and as she left she stopped and picked it up as a souvenir. As she got closer to the door, she felt that the pattern was getting hot, so hot she had to drop it. Once outside she and her friends examined her hand and found that it was red, as if it had been burned.

The directions to Lantern's Lane are also interesting. Once again, follow *u.s.* Route 24 out of Kentland for a short fifteen-mile drive to the never-ending world of Lantern's Lane. When you reach the city of Watseka, turn south on South Second Street and follow it out of town toward Woodland. This becomes State Route 1 and is known as Body Road! The Body Cemetery is on your right. Go west at the cemetery, then immediately turn south on 1980 East. This road will curve twice. After the second curve, turn west onto 1200 North. You will arrive at Lantern's Lane. All that's left of the house is a mailbox embedded in a stone post.

Cemeteries are common spots for reports of ghosts and paranormal activities, and Kentland-area cemeteries are no exception. One of the locals' favorite cemeteries to visit is located east of the village of Woodland, not too far past the state line. It is said that this cemetery was placed on top of an ancient Indian burial ground. As with all haunted sites, the best time to visit this site is when it's dark—if you dare. There you will find "Alfonso's Grave." This grave site is different from the others—it glows. Many believe the glowing is caused by a mysterious force from beyond.

From Sheldon, once again take "the ghost road" west to Route 1 south and turn west. Travel a short distance to County Road 2200 East. Follow this road south for approximately two miles and then turn east onto County Road 1550 North. Take the first right turn onto County Road 2290 East. Just after this turn, you will see a house off to the left and a small hill in the road.

Drive very slowly up this small hill. Look forward and to the right. As you pass the crest of the hill, you will see Alfonso's Grave. The other graves are not visible from the hill. You won't need to get out of the car to know you're at the right spot. Indeed, you probably wouldn't want to. There, before you in your headlights, will stand what appears to be the glowing figure of a man—

Alfonso! The figure will not move; it is just the glowing tomb-stone. Maybe.

Some theorize that this is just an anomaly that can be explained: They say the material the stone was made from coupled with the angle of the headlights, which produces the shape of a glowing man.

The final Kentland tale is a story about a haunted house and buried treasure. The Chidester family lived on a farm just outside of Kentland. They had one daughter, Mary Celesta. Mary died on September 18, 1922, when she was just nineteen. She is buried in Kentland's Fairlawn Cemetery along with her parents. For several years the family unsuccessfully tried to sell the farm. The house had a balcony over the entranceway, and each time prospective buyers visited the farm, they always asked about the girl in the brown dress standing on the balcony. The family never saw the girl that everyone else claimed to see.

Speculations and rumors began to spread that a treasure was buried on the farm and Mary Celesta was protecting it. Each time potential buyers were on the premises, Mary Celesta would appear to scare them off and away from the treasure.

After several years, the old house was torn down and a new one was built in its place. The barn with the Chidester name on its side still stands. Mary hasn't been seen for some time. Perhaps she feels it's no longer necessary to haunt the farm to protect the buried treasure. Maybe the treasure was just folklore. But there was a ghost.

PULASKI COUNTY

❖❖❖❖❖❖❖❖❖ ORIGINATED IN 1839, Pulaski County was named in honor of Polish Gen. Casimir Pulaski, a hero of the American Revolution who died at the attack of Savannah in 1779. Winamac, the county seat founded in 1839, was named for the Potawatomi chief Wi-na-mak, meaning "catfish."

In the 1930s, the Work Progress Administration (WPA) developed more than six thousand acres of recreational and wildlife property bordering on the Tippecanoe River. Approximately three hundred men worked on the project and were paid forty cents per hour. A part of this project became the Tippecanoe River State Park, established in 1943 with trails leading through oak forests and sand dunes. The Indiana Audubon Society recognizes this area as a significant site for spotting and cataloging various migrating bird species not normally associated with water.

The 1894 Romanesque-style courthouse in Winamac drew national attention during the 1980 Ford Pinto trials. The Ford Motor Company was accused of causing death by manufacturing a defective fuel tank system when a 1973 Pinto exploded on impact, killing three teenagers. Although the verdict found Ford not guilty of reckless homicide, the ten-week historic legal battle established that a corporation could be held criminally liable for faulty products.

Originally called Buena Vista, the village of Monterey was laid out in 1849. The name was changed to Monterey because there was already a Buena Vista in Indiana lo-cated in Jefferson County. Both names are derived from Mexican War battle sites. Just west of Monterey, a 1980 archaeological dig unearthed a ten-thousand-year-old mastodon skeleton. Once weighing more than two tons and measuring nineteen feet long, the remains are now the property of the Indiana State Museum in Indianapolis. ❖

The Praying Nun

Located in the northeast corner of Pulaski County is the little town of Monterey, population 231. This quiet, close-knit community has not made history, but it does have a mystery unique to its residents—a ghostly mystery.

The locals call the ghost the "Praying Nun." She appears at night in or near two Catholic cemeteries, Old Saint Anne's and New Saint Anne's, one northwest of Monterey and the other west of the town. They say a mysterious light can be seen moving late at night in either of the cemeteries.

According to local tradition, the glow emanates from Saint Anne's halo as she walks through the cemetery carrying a baby. Many years ago the baby was abandoned, left to die alone. Ever since the ghost of Saint Anne found the poor babe, she has cradled it in her arms each night.

If you enter the cemetery and see the Praying Nun's halo glowing in the dark, the locals say you will hear the baby crying.

Several school-aged children who have heard the story of the Praying Nun are convinced that they have seen her—but not in the cemeteries. There's an old barn situated close to a winding road near the oldest cemetery northwest of town. The children say on certain nights they've seen the outline of the nun on top of the barn, praying.

TIPPECANOE COUNTY

❖❖❖❖❖❖❖❖❖ ORGANIZED IN 1826, the county is named for the Tippecanoe River. The river's name is a form of the Potawatomi word "Ke-tap-e-kon-nong," which was the name of the Indian town located at the mouth of the river. Through humorous folklore many people think the name recalls an incident in which an Indian "tipped a canoe."

The founder of Lafayette was William Digby, a river boatman who realized that its location was ideal because it was the farthest a steamboat could navigate up the river. He purchased the land and platted the town in 1825, naming it after the Marquis de Lafayette, who was touring the United States at the time. The following year it was designated as the county seat.

In August of 1859, the city became the site for the first official United States postal service air-mail flight. John Wise took off in his balloon, the Jupiter, with a mail pouch containing several letters and circulars. The flight ended near Crawfordsville, approximately six hours after takeoff. Although that was not the intended destination, the flight was officially recognized.

Tippecanoe County's Purdue University is one of sixty-eight land-grant colleges founded under the provisions of the Morrill Act of 1862. Founded in 1869, classes began in 1874 with an enrollment of thirty-nine male students and a staff of six teachers.

In 1935, aviatrix Amelia Earhart became a visiting faculty member with the title of Consultant on Women's Careers. In 1937 the Purdue Research Foundation ac-quired the Lockheed 10-E Electra, which would enable her to fulfill her dream of circumnavigating the globe by air. At the conclusion of the flight, the Electra was to be returned to Purdue for exhibit. Unfortunately Amelia Earhart and the plane disappeared without a trace.

Also of note in the county is Tippecanoe Battlefield State Memorial and National Historic Landmark, located just northeast of Lafayette. It was the site of the first major conflict between Indians and whites in the Old Northwest since the Battle of Fallen Timbers in 1794.

It also was the site of the battle that began early on the morning of November 7, 1811, when approximately seven hundred Indians—made up of a confederation of Potawatomi, Shawnee, Kickapoo, Delaware, Winnebago, Wea, and Wyandotte tribes under directions of the Prophet, Chief Tecumseh's half-brother—attacked an encampment of nine hundred men under the command of Territorial Governor William Henry Harrison. Harrison's troops were able to repel the surprise attack, and the outcome resulted in the Prophet's loss of power within the Indian confederation. The battlefield, in May 1840, was the site chosen for presidential candidate William Henry Harrison to launch his successful campaign. As a result, the battle became immortalized by Harrison's campaign slogan of "Tippecanoe and Tyler Too."

The small town of Battleground was established near the 1811 battle site in 1858. Wolf Park is located about two miles outside of Battleground. This is a nonprofit education and research facility established in 1972 by Dr. Erich Klinghammer of Purdue University to allow scientists and students to observe and record the habits of wolves. Dedicated to education, research, and conservation, the park provides interpretive programs to school groups throughout the year and is open to the general public from May through November, and Saturday evenings for Howl Nights. ❖

"Baby Alice"

In 1875 the *Lafayette Journal* reported sightings of a strange bluish light floating about the yard of a house located at Thirteenth and Elizabeth Streets. When the house was dark, the bluish light reportedly appeared in the windows, floated out of the house, wandered about the yard, and then returned inside once again. What was the cause of this eerie occurrence?

For some time now, the house had been a notorious brothel. One of the "ladies" was known as "Baby Alice." All of the regulars knew no other name for her. Baby Alice must've been quite popular and well known, for when she became ill and finally died, an article appeared in the newspaper stating that her death was caused by "congestion of the lungs, produced by debauchery and exposure."

But what did her death have to do with the bluish light seen roaming in the brothel's windows and about the yard? Some of the witnesses to this phenomenon believed that the light resembled Baby Alice and that in her hands she carried a pitcher. Others swore it was Baby Alice, but that she wasn't carrying a pitcher in her hands—it was her heart and lungs.

Neighbors tried everything from magic potions to shotguns to stop the apparition. The madam and other women of the house were so upset by Alice's death and—reappearances—they hurriedly abandoned the it, leaving behind furniture and personal belongings. The house was put up for sale by the owner, who promised it would never again be used as a brothel.

After the madam and her "girls" left, the sightings of Baby Alice carrying her heart and lungs in her hands ceased. Perhaps she packed up and left with her co-workers.

It is hard to say if today the house is still there, since the newspaper only referred to the intersection. An elementary school is about a block away with its playground extending toward the intersection. The rest of the neighborhood is small residential homes, mostly rentals.

White Wolf

Ghost stories have been few and far between in the 179-year history of Lafayette, but perhaps the most notable story was reported
in the June 1872 issue of the *Evening Courier* and retold in the
Lafayette Leader. The *Courier* began as a weekly in 1845. Within
four years it became a daily publication under the leadership of
William S. Lingle. Many considered it to be one of Indiana's most
influential papers.

In the summer of 1872 a *Courier* reporter wrote a two-part story
titled "Among the Spirits." This was a "true" account of the most
fantastic supernatural events experienced by William Lingle and
guests in his home overlooking the Wabash Valley, located on Lingle
Avenue. The guests were Judge B.K. Higginbotham of the county
criminal court and three visitors, a Professor Amos S. Dillington
from London, and two men from Eastern Indiana papers.

During a congenial evening among friends, the conversation
turned toward the supernatural, in which they all had a mutual interest. Lingle shared the story of a supposedly haunted house located on
the site of an abandoned brickyard "at the head of North Street and
extending eastward half a mile past the city limits." The one-and-
a-half story structure, its windows missing, had two ground-floor
rooms and no closets—nor, it was assumed, any secret passages.

The five men decided to see the house for themselves. It was
about half past eight in the evening of June 20 when they arrived at
their destination. After surveying the exterior, they decided to enter
the house in the hope of scaring up a ghost or two. After looking
around the first floor, to make certain there weren't any secret passages, the gentlemen settled down to quietly wait. It was around ten
o'clock when an eerie blue-white light entered the room. The light
hovered like a cloud, then burned bright white and began taking the
shape of a white wolf!

The wolf seemed unaware of the men cowering in a corner of
the room. It trotted and ran about, finally stopping to raise its head
and utter a most frightful howl.

The men were transfixed by both curiosity and fear as they watched the apparition begin to transform again—this time into the shape of an indescribable creature. The body was like that of a big frog, with jaws like an alligator's, and a tail like a kangaroo's. The creature seemed to be suspended in mid-air for about five minutes or so, then changed into a cloud-like form that took the shape of an Indian holding a tomahawk in one hand and a torch in the other. Without a word or visible acknowledgment of the five men watching him, the Indian walked out into the open air and vanished.

The men returned to Lingle's home to retrieve a box Dillington had brought with him to the party. Then they returned to the haunted house, and Dillington removed a telescoping metal wand from the box. The professor, who had some knowledge of magic, used the wand to draw a circle in the dirt on the floor.

According to Lingle the circle measured more than seven feet. Dillington then divided this into sections in which he drew a series of mystical signs. Next, in the middle of the circle he sat a small tripod and a lamp. The lamp's flame burned an eerie green and emitted a most foul smell.

Not knowing what to think or say, the other men watched in fascination as an Indian dressed in war costume appeared from out of the flame and smoke. Dillington calmly communicated with the Indian in a tongue that was not known to the others. After a few minutes, Dillington turned to his companions and translated the conversation between himself and the Indian.

The Indian's name in life had been "White Wolf." He bore a tattoo on his right arm in the shape of the frog-like creature they'd seen earlier. This beast, according to Indian legends, once abounded in western rivers. White Wolf told of being buried in an Indian cemetery on the Longlois reservation northeast of Lafayette, only to have his spirit disturbed by the shovels of those building the city.

Needless to say, the Courier's articles were the talk of the town—and out of town, as well. The paper received a number of letters recounting other strange encounters with the supernatural. One of these letters came from a resident of Linnwood, at the northeast edge of Lafayette. He had an employee of Indian heritage who had spoken many times to the spirit of White Wolf. The employee said that White Wolf would never rest until a fence was built around the Spring Vale Cemetery.

After the initial excitement concerning these articles, there seemed to be no other record of White Wolf ever being seen, heard, or experienced again.

According to Robert Kriebel, *Courier* staff writer, the location of the haunted house was situated, by its 1872 description, half a mile east of the city limits on North Street, past Barbee's Grove. The city limits in 1872 ended at about Eighteenth Street. Barbee's Grove is the hilltop growth of trees known today as Murdock Park. The abandoned brickyard and the haunted house evidently stood to the east of Murdock Park, possibly in the general vicinity of today's Sunnyside Junior High.

Did this actually happen? Five respected gentlemen, one of them the owner and editor of the newspaper, swore that it had.

WABASH COUNTY

❖❖❖❖❖❖❖❖❖❖ ORGANIZED IN 1835 and named for the Wabash, the principal Indiana river, Wabash is a contraction of the Miami word "Wah-bah-shik-ki." In 1827, the settlement of Wabash Town was established as the county seat. Two years later, a post office was established and named Treaty Grounds. Hugh Hanna and David Burr, the first Treaty Grounds postmaster, platted the city in 1834. The name of Treaty Grounds was changed in 1839 to Wabash, and at that time Hanna became postmaster.

A cemetery of note is the Frances Slocum/Bundy Cemetery. Frances Slocum was born in 1773. Three Delaware Indians attacked her family's home in Wilkes-Barre, Pennsylvania, in 1778, when she was only five years old. Frances was taken by the Indians and assimilated into the Delaware nation. Eventually she was adopted by a childless couple who called her Weketaswash.

The family and tribe settled in the Miami village of Kekionga, near present-day Fort Wayne. She was married to the Miami war chief Shepoconah in the early 1790s and adopted the Miami name, Maconaqua, "Little Bear Woman." Shepoconah died in 1833, but Maconaqua and her two daughters remained with the Miami.

Slocum's family never gave up the search for Frances and in 1837 they found her. She chose to stay, however, with her adopted race. She died in 1847. She was buried beside her husband, Shepoconah, in the Bundy Cemetery in Miami County. The name was changed in 1900 to Frances Slocum Cemetery when descendents erected a monument to her memory. After the creation of the Mississinewa Lake, the cemetery was moved in the late

1960s to Wabash County.

Wabash city also earned fame as the first municipally electric-lighted city in the world. In February 1880 the Common Council agreed to let the Brush Electric Light Company install four Brush electric arc lights on the courthouse tower. At twilight on March 31 the lights went on in Wabash. The lights could be seen five miles from town.

One of the most influential citizens born in Wabash was Mark C. Honeywell (1874–1964). At the turn of the century he established a heating contracting business. The Honeywell Heating Specialties Company, founded in 1902, specialized in developing automatically controlled heating. The company merged with his chief competitor in 1927 to form Minneapolis-Honeywell Regulator Company, which became Honeywell, Inc., in 1964. Today it's one of the largest U.S. businesses with plants throughout the world.

Hanging Rock is a unique natural formation, jutting eighty-four feet above the Wabash River. Once a part of a Silurian coral reef covered by prehistoric oceans, the flat-topped rock provides an ideal observation point to see the Wabash and Salamonie rivers and surrounding countryside.

One of Wabash County's most famous citizens is author Gene Stratton Porter. Her father, Mark Stratton, a Methodist minister, was one of the founders of the Hopewell Church located near the city of Wabash. This was also the site of the Stratton farm where Gene was born. In 1872 Gene's brother, Leander, drowned in the Wabash River and was buried in Hopewell Church Cemetery. Leander served as the model for the title character in Porter's 1913 novel, *Laddie*.

The town of North Manchester, platted in 1837, was home to the DeWitt automobile. From 1908–1913, V.L. DeWitt manufactured automobiles with solid rubber tires and forty-inch diameter spoke wheels made of hickory. A replica is on display at the North Manchester Historical Society.

North Manchester is also the birthplace of Thomas R. Marshall (1854–1925). He became governor of Indiana (1909–1913) and the twenty-eighth Vice President of the United States (1913–1921) during the Woodrow Wilson administration. His childhood home, built in 1848, originally stood at 126 East Main Street, but it was moved several times before reaching its present location in 1898 at 409 North Market Street. Marshall returned to his hometown in 1925 to give the commencement address at Manchester College. Ten days later he died.

Manchester College had its beginning in 1860 as the Roanoke Classical Seminary, founded by the United Brethren Church. The name was changed when the seminary moved to North Manchester in 1889. Gradually the school evolved into a liberal arts college. Today the student body is made up of all faiths.

A 1931 graduate of Manchester College, Paul J. Flory (1910–1985) received the 1974 Nobel laureate in chemistry for his achievements, both theoretical and experimental, in the physical chemistry of the macromolecules. In his acceptance speech he readily acknowledged that his science education at Manchester sparked his life-long interests in scientific research. ❖

The Legend of Hanging Rock

About a mile southeast of Lagro, rising eighty-four feet above the Wabash River near the mouth of the Salamonie River, is a remnant of a huge reef known as Hanging Rock. The rock is more than four hundred million years old.

At the summit is a flat space some twenty feet square that commands a broad outlook over the river and valley below. The rock historically has played a significant role in the lives of the inhabitants of the area, as it still does today. Many young people climb the same pathway to the top that Miami Indian braves and maidens climbed many years before them.

In his book, *Miami Indian Stories,* Chief Clarence Godfroy tells of a beautiful Indian maiden who jumped to her death from this spot. It is rumored that some people who have ventured there on lonesome evenings have seen the ghostly image of the Indian maiden leap from the hanging stone.

Her name was Wy-nu-sa, a beautiful Miami Indian maiden who was in love with two handsome, strong, and stalwart braves. And they, in turn, were deeply in love with her. When asked to choose between the two, the beautiful maiden could not decide which brave she wanted to marry. She concluded that they would have to prove their worth. To the two young suitors Wy-nu-sa said, "You will have to fight a duel at the top of Hanging Rock. At that time I will sit and wait for the brave who wins the fight to come to me. He, I will marry. The brave who loses the duel will fall to his death in the swirling waters of the river below the rock."

The two young men agreed to the challenge. They chose a night with a full moon, and when it arrived, the two young braves climbed to the top of Hanging Rock to fight for the love of the Indian maiden. Wy-nu-sa also climbed to the top and stood in the shadows to watch the fight. She loved one of the braves more than the other, but she wouldn't admit this to anyone, not even to herself.

The two braves were equally matched. The duel was fought long into the night. Clouds began to drift across the moon while the battle raged on. As the clouds drifted past the face of the full moon, the rock was illuminated just as one brave fell over the edge and plunged to his death below.

The victor came over to Wy-nu-sa to claim her as his bride. When she saw the brave, she screamed out in anguish, "I do not love you!

You have killed my own true love. I cannot live without him!"

She then ran to the edge of the rock and threw herself into the water below to join her true love in death. The Miami Indians be-lieve she is now with her brave in the happy hunting grounds.

However, many believe the drama is repeated by the spirits of the maiden and her braves. Wy-nu-sa's story has not only been immortalized in Miami legend and folklore of Wabash County but in a ballad titled "The Ballad of Hanging Rock," written by Story Sellers.

A view of Hanging Rock from below.
PHOTO: Jonathan Tétreault

Moonrock

Two miles west of Wabash there's a giant boulder, a type of rock known as a pudding stone, containing particles of varying sized granite, gneiss, and sienite.

The Moonrock, as the boulder is known, is located off old *u.s.* Route 24 west of Wabash, and is situated snugly between two large trees. It rises six feet above the ground, fifteen feet long and twelve feet wide. Geologists believe that it is the largest of its kind in the state. The stone is not native to Indiana, but came from the north shore of Lake Superior transported by the power of glacial activities. Other boulders lay nearby, but this huge rock commands attention.

Chief Clarence Godfroy, in *Miami Indian Stories,* describes this rock and the importance it held to the Miami Indians. They honored the rock as a relic of the battles of the gods, esteeming it as a holy altar where they left offerings of wampum and tobacco to maintain the gods' good favors.

The huge rock, with its variety of embedded colored stones, would shimmer in the light of a full moon. Thus, the Miami worshiped it as in connection with their moon god. As the moon rose they came to this place several times a week to dance and perform rituals to honor the moon god.

According to legend, the magic of the Moonrock is still evident as it shimmers in the light of a full moon. Throughout the years, witnesses have claimed to see the shadowy figures of Indian dancers from long ago. But that's only their imagination—or is it?

Moonrock and a ghostly orb that was visible only to the camera's lens.
PHOTO: Jonathan Tétreault

CENTRAL
INDIANA

BOONE COUNTY

✦✦✦✦✦✦✦✦✦✦ BOONE, ORGANIZED IN 1830, was the state's sixty-third county. The county was named for the famous frontiersman, Daniel Boone. Lebanon, the county seat, was platted in 1832 and named for the biblical mountains.

According to legend, Boone County had a reputation of being one of the swampiest in the state. Every night from early spring through the summer, the frogs created a constant dull roar. The inhabitants got accustomed to it, and after a while didn't even hear it. The story started circulating in the surrounding counties that people who lived in Boone County had webbed feet! When "Boonites" visited another county, they could expect to be asked to show everybody their feet.

On May 1, 1831, the commissioners convened to de-cide on a name for the county seat. According to local tradition, A.M. French, the youngest of the commissioners, was gazing at the tall trees around him when he thought of the biblical cedars of Lebanon and shouted "Lebanon." Another tradition, however, says he chose the name of the city in honor of his hometown in Ohio.

Picturesque Zionsville is today a tourist destination. In the 1960s the business district was remodeled to resemble a New England village. Main Street was paved with bricks and decorated with planters and gas lamps. Nineteenth-century homes have been converted into antique shops, boutiques, and restaurants. Newer buildings are designed to blend with the older style of architecture.

Zionsville, settled around 1830, was platted adjacent to the Cincinnati, Indianapolis, and the Lafayette Railroad in 1852, and was named for the surveyor, William Zion.

A railroad station once stood in the general vicinity of the southwest corner of Cedar and First Streets, which is now occupied by the tiny Lincoln Memorial Park. A marker was placed on this site by the Lions Club to commemorate February 11, 1861, the day Abraham Lincoln's train stopped on its way to Washington and he addressed the citizens of Zionsville.

Located on State Route 39 in Lebanon is another marker erected in 1966 by the Indiana Sesquicentennial Committee of Boone County, which also commemorates Lincoln's train stopping there.

The Boone County courthouse, completed in 1911, was designed and constructed by Caldwell and Drake of Columbus. The building has an eighty-four-foot-high and fifty-two-foot-wide dome, the second largest in the state. The thirty-five-foot-tall hand-cut monolithic columns at the north and south entrances are believed to be the largest single-piece pillars in the nation. The courthouse has been placed on the National Register of Historic Places.

Prior to the platting of Thorntown in 1831, a French trading post was established in 1720 near the Miami village Ka-wi-a-ki-un-gi, meaning "place of thorns."

There are several variants on the legend of how Thorntown got its name. One of the most colorful tells of two young warriors who competed for the hand of a beautiful Indian maiden and killed each other. The heartbroken princess pierced her heart with a thorn from the bushes that grew in the area; thus, the village came to be known as the "place of thorns." ✤

The Screaming Road

It was 1951. They were young. Still in High School. Going steady. He had his first car. They were out on a date just driving around when he turned onto Road 334 between Zionsville and Eagle Village and headed for "lovers' lane."

Many of the students at their high school knew of this location and often went there to do a little innocent "necking." It was quiet and secluded and safe. Or it had been.

What happened is still a mystery. Perhaps they were sitting in the car listening to the radio when something outside the car startled them. Did they hear a sound and get out of the car to investigate? Or did someone open the door and grab the girl? All that is known is that the two teens ended up dead.

No one remembers exactly when or how the bodies were found—only their condition. Both bodies were found under a tree beside the road, bloodied and mangled—apparently victims of an ax murderer. The boy probably was killed first trying desperately to defend his girlfriend. The girl was believed to have been brutally raped and then chopped to pieces. They both must have put up a valiant fight for their lives, but in vain. The killer, surely a madman, was never found.

For some time, young lovers stayed away from the area out of respect—and fear. Finally, time erased the fear, and couples once again began to turn onto Road 334 and headed for the lovers' lane. Those who have braved the area occasionally have reported hearing sounds—sounds of a young boy and girl screaming. The sounds always seemed to come from near a huge tree. Could it be the same tree where the two mangled bodies had been found?

If you dare to search for lovers' lane on Road 334, you, too, might hear the screams.

CLINTON COUNTY

❖❖❖❖❖❖❖❖❖ THIS COUNTY was organized in 1830 and named for New York governor De Witt Clinton. The county seat, Frankfort, was laid out in 1830, and probably named for Frankfurt. A.M. Main, Germany, home to the grandfather of the Pence brothers, who owned the land on which the city is located; however, some believe the town was named for Kentucky's state capital.

Frankfort's Kemp Brothers Packing Company (later Del Monte, which is no longer located in Frankfort) claimed to have marketed the country's first commercially canned tomato juice in 1928.

The National Cigar Corporation is located in a three-story brick building on the northeast corner of Frankfort's Main Street. The operation was started by Noah Smith in 1919. Smith later sold out to the John Burger and Son Company, and the National Cigar Corporation was formed.

Another industry located in the Frankfort area is Frito Lay, which built the world's largest salty snack food facility in 1980.

The home of the Clinton County Historical Society Museum is located in "Old Stony." This former high and junior high school building, built in 1892, represents a rare combination of several architectural styles projecting a castle-like appearance. The building receives its nickname from its sandstone exterior. Among those Frankfort natives who attended high school in "Old Stony" was late actor Will Geer (1912–1978).

Geer made his acting debut in 1928. By the late 1940s, he had become a character actor in films, often appearing

in Westerns, such as *Comanche Territory* and
Director Otto Preminger cast him as a Senate minority
leader in *dvise and Consent*. He often appeared on televi-
sion in shows ranging from *Gunsmoke to Hawaii Five-O*
Perhaps he's best known though as Grandpa (Zebulon)
Walton in the '70s television series *The Waltons*. ❖

The "De-ghoster" Twins

Long before the hit movie *Ghostbusters,* Frankfort, Indiana, had its
own team of ghostbusters, twins Rolland and Oliver Woollen.
During an *Indianapolis Monthly* interview in 1984, the twins
claimed that in their sixty years of "de-ghosting," they'd "piled up
more than five hundred success stories."

For these retired twin truckers, ghosthunting was more of a
pastime than a profession, though they charged a flat fee of $1,500
for their services. This might have seemed somewhat steep, but
the Woollen twins guaranteed their work. One of the twins stated,
"When we work (de-ghost) a house, it stays that way." They knew
what they were doing. According to the twins, no job of de-ghosting took longer than fifteen minutes.

How did these twins become successful ghosthunters? When
they were twelve years old, they were taught their skills by a woman
they referred to as a "near aunt." The Woollen twins both agree
that most ghosts aren't dangerous, only bothersome. They admitted, though, poltergeists can be "a touch aggravating."

They'd never personally seen more than two or three ghosts,
although they had experienced the handiwork of such entities or
had seen their share of "weird things." One of these "weird things"
took place in a house where the daughter would make her bed in
the morning and then return that evening only to find it messed up.
When she got in the bed, she reported feeling like someone else
was getting in with her. Of course, her parents wanted this to stop

and called on the de-ghoster duo. Evidently they were successful, for the family never needed to contact them again after that one time.

One of the Woollens' favorite de-ghosting stories concerned the unsolved murder of a miner who walked with a peg leg after losing his leg in a mining accident. One day he was found dead in a room on the second floor of his home. The murder was never solved. The new owners often heard what they described as the sound of someone with a peg leg pacing through the second-floor rooms. After a visit by the Woollens, the pegged-leg pacing was no longer heard.

The twins' de-ghosting fame and activities were not confined to Clinton County. They once were requested to visit a Marion County home in Broadripple to de-ghost a house that the Woollens be-lieved to have been built on the site where an Indian mother and her baby had died. Their spirits were felt throughout the house by its current residents—and the twins knew just how to handle it.

As the Woollen brothers aged, they considered passing their se-crets on to someone they could trust—someone who would continue de-ghosting. A young man from Frankfort indicated he was interested, so they took him with them on one of their jobs. According to the Woollens he was a "big fella. You know, the kind who could eat baled hay and pull a wagon." When asked how he did, the brothers snickered. "Couldn't get him out of the car." Thus, the brothers' de-ghosting secrets went to the graves with them.

The Ghosts of Sleepy Hollow

Washington Irving's *The Legend of Sleepy Hollow* is a permanent part of our literary history. The town of Sleepy Hollow along with the headless horseman have become part of our national folklore.

The spirit that haunts Irving's Sleepy Hollow is the ghost of a Hessian trooper who has been decapitated by a cannonball during a Revolutionary War scrimmage. He rides wildly through the countryside at night seeking his head, but must return to his burial site before daybreak.

Indiana has its own Sleepy Hollow located just outside of Frankfort, and it, too, has a haunting tale. You won't encounter a headless horseman, but what they say you'll find there is much more frightening. Clinton County's Sleepy Hollow is located on a lonely road near a bridge spanning the South Fork of Wildcat Creek.

The story has its origin sometime in the 1800s. A farmer's wife had just prepared and served the evening meal. No one knows why it happened or how it happened, but the seemingly docile wife had killed her husband. Had she taken all she could from a domineering, demanding man? Or had she simply gone mad? Did she use her iron skillet to end his life?

To cover up the crime and dispose of the evidence—the body—she decided to cut him up into manageable pieces. Once this was achieved, she waited until it was dark. Then she loaded him onto the wagon and proceeded to Wildcat Creek bridge. Once there she began to toss him, piece by piece, over the bridge and into the creek.

Later, she became fearful that someone would find the pieces. Night after night she went to the bridge to make certain there was nothing to be found. Even if she wasn't out of her mind when she killed her husband, her guilt most certainly drove her insane. In fact, even after her death, she still protects her secret.

Many have said that on this lonely road as you approach the bridge, she'll appear as a light floating toward you in an attempt to scare you away. But if you're really "lucky," according to some stories you might encounter the husband rising from the creek—piece by piece.

To find Sleepy Hollow, follow these directions—if you dare. Take State Route 28 west out of Frankfort until you reach West Mulberry-Jefferson Road. Turn right and follow the road until you come to 600-West. Continue on 600-West until you see the bridge—and perhaps something else.

Wildcat Creek bridge, which lies in Indiana's own Sleepy Hollow.
PHOTO: Eric L. Mundell

DELAWARE COUNTY

❖❖❖❖❖❖❖❖❖❖ THIS COUNTY WAS orga-
nized in 1827 and named for the Delaware indians, who
had villages in the area from 1720 to 1818. Muncie, the
county seat, was settled as early as 1818 and platted in
1827. The name was derived from the Munsee band of
Delawares who lived in the area. The name of the band,
Min-si or Min-thi-u (sometimes spelled Monsy and
Monthee), means "people of the stony country."

The state's gas industry began here with the discovery
of natural gas in 1876. Exploring for coal near Eaton, ten
miles north of Muncie, drillers struck natural gas. No
effort was made to capitalize on this find because natural
gas had little economic worth at the time. The realization
of the energy potential of natural gas led to the reopening
of the Eaton well in 1886. Two years later Delaware
County had thirty-five producing wells. Companies requir-
ing high levels of heat in manufacturing, such as glass,
iron, and steel, flocked to the area.

After a fire destroyed his family's glass canning jar factory in 1886, Frank C. Ball moved the business from Buffalo, New York, to Muncie to take advantage of the cheap
and plentiful fuel supply. Frank Ball and his brother became
involved in what today is known as Ball State University.

Eventually the "inexhaustible" supply of natural gas
began to dwindle. Luckily, Muncie's economic welfare did
not rest solely on the availability of natural gas. Oil had
been discovered along with gas, and it continued to be
pumped for several years.

Muncie's post-gas-boom economy was paralleled by
efforts to establish a college that would add a cultural
dimension to the industrialized community. The backers

for this proposed institution included the Ball brothers. A sixty-four-acre location was acquired for the school. The University Building (now Ball State's Administration Building) was completed in 1899, and the Eastern Indiana Normal University established for the education of males and females opened with an initial enrollment of 232. The school lasted only two years. Several other schools located on the site.

In 1918 the Ball brothers purchased the sixty-four acres with its two buildings and presented them to the state. The Eastern Division of the Indiana State Normal School at Muncie, a branch of the State Normal School at Terre Haute, opened in June of that year. Four years later the state legislature honored the Ball family's generosity by changing the school's name to Ball Teachers College, Eastern Division, Indiana State Normal School. The school separated from the Terre Haute institution in 1929 and became Ball State Teachers College. It achieved university status in 1965 with the name changed to Ball State University. Through their philanthropic activities and dedication to education, the Ball family, industrial and community leaders, have left an indelible mark on Muncie.

Christy Woods is the oldest developed nature preserve among the several operated by Ball State. The seventeen-acre tract is situated west of the Cooper Science Building on Riverside Avenue. The nature laboratory is named for Dr. Otto B. Christy, a member of the science faculty (1918– 1950) who was largely responsible for furbishing the ar-boretum in the 1930s. Used for student recreation and biology field studies, the woods have walking paths and gardens that are open to the public.

Within this area are the two greenhouses, established in 1971, that contain the Wheeler Orchid Collection and

Species Bank. This is considered to be the world's largest collection of orchids. Dedicated to conservation and education, Wheeler maintains over eighty-five genera, represented by over five hundred different species and over one hundred hybrid orchids.

During the early twentieth century, automobile makers helped diversify Muncie's economy. At least seven makes of cars were produced in the city between 1908 and 1928. William C. Durant, who organized General Motors in 1908 and lost control in 1920, founded the Durant Motors Company in 1921. Located in Muncie, Durant's company manufactured the Princeton, the Star, and the Durant.

Humorist-author Emily Kimbrough was born in Muncie in 1898. The future editor of the *Ladies Home Journal* and author of seventeen books spent her first eleven years in a two-story frame house at 715 East Washington Street. Today, her home is the centerpiece of a twelve-block area of Victorian-era homes designated in 1978 as the Emily Kimbrough historic District. Two of her most familiar works are *Our Hearts Were Young and Gay* (1942), co-authored with Cornelia Otis Skinner, and *How Dear to My Heart* (1944), the story of growing up in Muncie during the early years of the twentieth century. ❖

Ball State Student Keeps Hanging Around

Ball State University's 1,036-acre residential campus located in Muncie began in 1899 as a private two-year school for teaching elementary teachers. The campus and buildings were purchased by the Ball brothers, Muncie industrialists, and given to the state of Indiana in 1916. The institution became a university in 1965.

A campus tour gives prospective students an insight into a university still young in its history—and leaves them equally capti-vated by the facts and folklore their tour guides share.

The group pauses at the "academic mascot of the university," the winged Beneficence, a female sculpture fondly called "Benny" by Ball State students. This was the last work of Daniel Chester French, who also created Lincoln Memorial in the nation's capital. The tour guide explains one of the meanings behind Benny's gestures. Her left hand holds a treasure chest, which represents all of the knowl-edge and wealth gained through an education at Ball State. Her right hand is reaching out to help students achieve those goals.

Those in the group also learn that Benny is a part of the campus folklore legends. It is widely known by Ball State students and alumni that if you kiss the one you love underneath Beneficence—keeping your eyes closed, of course—and you are meant to be to-gether, she will flap her wings. The legend has never been dis-puted. What one cannot see, one cannot deny.

As the group moves from one location to another, it leaves the essence of romance and history and moves on to the eeriness of a haunted dormitory. Elliott Hall was built in 1938. Even the con-struction provides a chilling story: The building was built by Frank C. Ball in memory of his son, Frank Elliott Ball. His son was attend-ing Princeton University in the late 1920s when he was killed in an airplane crash. According to legend Elliott Hall is an exact replica of the young man's dormitory at Princeton.

Elliott Hall also houses a dark and unsettling story, a legend that began just after World War *ii*. According to the story, a veteran injured during combat returned to his home in Indiana, enrolled at Ball State and became a resident of Elliott Hall. His injuries had left him horribly disfigured and partially crippled. It was difficult for him to adjust to civilian life, to accept his disfigurement and disabilities, and to cope with the stress of being a college student. He became despondent.

One night during a vacation break at Ball State, he left his room, climbed to the fourth floor, and hung himself from a rafter.

Residents of Elliott are certain that he still roams the building where he met his violent end. Perhaps because of his disfigurement he has not materialized, but many students claim to have sensed his presence.

HOWARD COUNTY

❖❖❖❖❖❖❖❖❖❖ ORGANIZED IN 1844, the county was originally named Richardville, for the famous Miami Chief Jean Baptiste Richardville. The name was changed to Howard in 1846 to honor Hoosier statesman and soldier Tilghman A. Howard.

The first settler in the county was David Faster. He arrived in 1842, obtained land from Chief LaFontaine, and established a trading post on what had been a Miami Indian reservation. In 1844 he laid out the town and named it for the Miami Chief Kokomoko (spellings vary). The town was chosen to be the county seat because of its central location and the fact that Faster donated the land for the courthouse.

The city became an industrial leader with the discovery of natural gas in 1886. According to tradition, Kokomo has two nicknames: "Stoplight City," because of its many stoplights, and "The City of Firsts," due to its many discoveries and inventions.

The most famous of the inventions was the creation of the first successful, gasoline-powered commercial automobile in Indiana. It was built in 1894 by Elwood Haynes (1858–1925). He also discovered stainless steel (1911) and "Stellite" (1906), a high-performance, nickel-chromium alloy.

Other Kokomo inventions included the pneumatic rubber tire (1894), the carburetor (1902), the American howitzer shell and aerial bomb with fins (1918), and the all-transistor push button car radio (1957). Fifteen major discoveries and inventions have taken place in Kokomo.

Elmer and Edgar Apperson established the Riverside Machine Shop in 1888. They assembled the first Haynes horseless carriage in 1894. Four years later, the Haynes-Apperson Company was incorporated. The Appersons withdrew from the company in 1901 and formed the Apperson Brothers Automobile Company, which re-mained in business until 1925. The Haynes Automobile Company filed for bankruptcy in October 1924 and dissolved the following February.

The Howard County Museum was originally the home of Monroe Seiberling, founder of the Diamond Plate Glass Company, forerunner of the Pittsburgh Plate Glass Company. The twenty-nine-room Neo-Jacobean and Romanesque revival-style home was built around 1890 at a cost of $50,000. In 1972 the mansion was placed on the list of National Register of Historic Places.

Highland Park, located off Deffenbagh Street, was es-tablished in 1892. In addition to the usual city park attractions, Highland also includes several noteworthy historical sites within its one hundred acres. The 117-foot Vermont Covered Bridge, built near the Howard County town of Vermont in 1875, was moved to the park in 1958. Two of the area's more unusual attractions are Old Ben and the Sycamore stump. In a shelter with white siding and a picture window stands Old Ben, a large stuffed steer. The crossbred Hereford was born in Miami County in 1902 and raised just north of Kokomo. At age four, the steer weighed 4,720 pounds, stood six feet-five-inches tall, was twenty-six-feet-eight-inches in length, and measured thirteen-feet-six-inches in girth. Ben was exhibited throughout the country before a broken leg forced his destruction in 1911. Next to Ben in a fenced shelter is a Sycamore stump that once was located on a farm near New London, southeast of Kokomo. The one hundred-foot-high tree was severely damaged by high winds and flooding in 1915. The stump, which is fifty-one feet in circumference and twelve feet high, was placed in the park in 1916. It was hollowed out and used as a phone booth. Twenty-four people at one time were able to fit in the stump booth.

Greentown, laid out in 1848 and incorporated in 1873, was named either for a patch of green meadow in the wilderness or for the Miami Indian town located on the site, which was called Green's Village after a Miami chief. The town grew with the gas boom. However, the town owes its long-standing national—if not international—fame to a tragic fire in 1903.

With the discovery of natural gas in the area, the Indiana Tumbler and Goblet Company was established in 1894. The company manufactured pressed glass tumblers, goblets, tableware, and souvenir glassware. The production of colored glass began in 1897, and two years later the company merged with nineteen companies to form the National Glass Company. Glass chemist Jacob Rosenthal came to Greentown in 1900. It was his un-usual color creations for which Greentown Glass re-ceived its national reputation. His best-known colored glass creations were chocolate brown and golden agate.

The Indiana Tumbler and Goblet factory was de-stroyed by fire in 1903. It was never rebuilt, nor were the molds and glass ever replicated. A Greentown Glass Museum was established in the old City Hall building in 1970, corresponding with the first annual Greentown Glass Festival. Nearly one thousand pieces of Greentown Glass are displayed in the museum. The Festival, which is held in early June, attracts thousands of visit-ors. Greentown Glass is now a highly sought after item by glass collectors throughout the United States and beyond. ❖

Jerome's Devil Dog

Jerome Cemetery sits on the east bank of Wildcat Creek, just west of Jerome on 150 South and 1000 East, a short distance east of Greentown. The first burials took place in 1846 and continued to the end of the nineteenth century. The medium-sized cemetery surrounded by trees is a well-hidden, quiet, and peaceful location. Or is it?

For a very long time, reports of strange sightings have circulated throughout the area. The more curious and daring residents have ventured out to see what lurks among the aging stones. Some individuals have described seeing a man in a dark cape standing in the middle of the cemetery along with a large black dog. More frequently, visitors have reported seeing a mysterious large black dog that seems not to be of this world.

Accounts of ethereal black dog sightings are not new. On the contrary, it is a large and complex part of supernatural folklore. Throughout England for hundreds of years, there have been accounts of "Devil Dog" encounters.

Perhaps the most famous of all of these is Sir Arthur Conan Doyle's *The Hound of the Baskervilles*. Although this is a work of fiction, he most likely based this story on England's Dartmoor myths. One of these tells of a mythical huntsman and his pack of evil, wild, red-eyed hounds that terrorizes the local countryside. The legend states that all who meet up with the dogs will die within one year. If the individuals attempt to follow the dogs, they will meet with immediate death. Yet another myth, which also could have inspired Doyle, describes a large black dog with flaming red eyes and a "satanic nature." It is said that the "Black Dog" guards specific lanes, gates, bridges, or cemeteries. Encountering these red-eyed creatures will result in a run for your life.

In several of the myths, the lone "Black Dog" is not as ferocious as either the pack or Doyle's hound of the Baskervilles. According to English legend, the lone "Black Dog" can be seen even on the darkest of nights because he is so much blacker than the night itself. He appears on the left of the observer, then crosses the road or path from left to right. Rather than a portent of death, he is portrayed as a spirit of protection. In several encounters, observers have claimed the distraction of the dog's appearance saved them from a life-threatening accident, such as a fall or car accident.

Is there any connected between the Dartmoor myths and what has been experienced in the Jerome Cemetery? The tales are similar and could support the far-reaching folkloric belief in big black spirit dogs, one malevolent, the other benevolent.

One of the local folklore stories says that the Jerome cemetery is haunted and that anyone entering after dark will be chased by a big black phantom dog with eyes glowing like fire. Once the person leaves the cemetery, the dog will suddenly disappear.

Another folklore story says that visitors who enter the graveyard during the night might encounter a man in a black cape standing in the middle of the cemetery with two big black dogs.

Yet another tale circulating in the area is that of an eyewitness encounter reported by the occupants of a car as they were driving on the road from the cemetery to the town of Jerome. The road was deserted except for their car. All of a sudden the occupants heard a dog barking so loudly it sounded as if it was right in the car. They stopped. The barking ceased, and then from the left side of

A headstone at Jerome Cemetery.
PHOTO: Peggy McClelland

the road they saw the red glowing eyes of a big black dog. Just at that moment, a large deer came crashing out of the darkness and across the road. If they had not stopped when they heard the dog barking, they surely would have hit the deer. They believed the dog had saved them from a potentially disastrous collision. When they looked back at the side of the road, the dog was gone.

Are there a devil dog and its master in Jerome Cemetery waiting to foretell your death? Or, is the dog residing in the cemetery a spirit protector?

Kokomo's Haunted Funeral Home

In 2000, a downtown Kokomo building that had once been a fu-neral home was purchased by a man and his wife who had plans to renovate and give it a new life. This was not unusual. What made this purchase unique was the share of folklore, legends—and ghosts—that came along with it.

The funeral home, located at 118-120 East Walnut Street, first began business in 1902 as Smith & Keller in rooms once occupied by the Sears Roebuck. In 1919 W. Earle Jacob joined the business as a partner. The firm continued operation at the East Walnut Street address until 1937, when it acquired a residence at 208 East Mulberry Street that the partners converted into a funeral home. It was enlarged and extensively remodeled in 1952.

When Smith died in December 1937, Jacob assumed full ownership. Two years later his son, George, became a partner. The father died in 1952. Jacob's Funeral Service continued for twenty years until George retired in 1972.

The building was then purchased by The Kokomo Tribune Realty Corporation. R.H. Blacklidge, publisher of the *Kokomo Tribune,* stated in a September 1972 article that the newspaper planned to convert the former funeral home into an adjunct of the Tribune's publishing business. This did not happen. The property had various tenants until it was sold in 2000.

The new owners, who have requested anonymity, are attempting to renovate the building for apartments and office space. They didn't realize how hard this was going to be. While they knew the physical work would be hard, they didn't count on encounters of the paranormal type to slow their progress.

Boxes of old and deteriorating funeral home records, newspapers, candlesticks and candles, along with other items connected with the funeral business, including embalming basins, were discovered in the basement and attic. Some of the boxes were marked "personal belongings" and contained old Bibles, glasses, jewelry, a gold wedding ring, and numerous other items, which they believed probably had been intended to be buried with the deceased. In the attic they also found furniture, old pictures and frames, and other miscellaneous items. The owners knew it would take them a lot of time to sort through everything that had been stored and forgotten.

But had it been forgotten? Could there be "someone" watching over these items all these years? Perhaps one of the original owners of these personal items?

In one of the rooms a picture of Jesus was discovered. The couple liked it and decided to give it to the husband's mother for Mother's Day since she was very religious and collected pictures of Jesus. She was delighted—at first.

The morning after receiving the picture from the funeral home she was about to enter her shower when she felt herself being pushed! She hit her head, sustaining a deep cut. The other strange thing about the incident was that the hot water was no longer hot. It was ice cold!

She felt the cut was bad enough that she should go to the hospital. The doctor asked what had happened. Knowing he wouldn't believe her if she told him a ghost had pushed her, she said she'd tripped and hit her head. After returning home she called her son and told him what had happened. He listened in disbelief. Yet she was convinced that something had pushed her in the shower. She wanted him to take the picture back because she felt certain it was possessed. The son was baffled but agreed to take the picture back to the funeral home.

But this was not the last of the mysterious events. The owners and others helping to renovate the building have seen black shadowy figures on numerous occasions. These shadow people are said to be seen during all hours. The wife seems to experience this phenomenon more frequently than her husband. Whispers have also been heard in the hallways, and footsteps on the stairs. Lights go out and come back on by themselves. Even water is affected—it, too, will inexplicably turn on or off by itself.

One day a worker told the owner he'd heard something in the basement that sounded like a high-pitched drilling noise. Their children have also reported seeing what they describe as "black fog" in several of the rooms. After the children began reporting sightings, the husband acknowledged that something strange was going on. But what?

To settle everybody's concerns, he sought out the assistance of a psychic. When the psychic heard what building was involved she adamantly refused to go there. Instead, she issued a warning to the man that he was stirring up trouble. She refused to answer questions about the shadow people had seen in the building and kept telling him that they needed to leave the building alone.

Jacob Funeral home, where "shadow people" roam the halls. PHOTO: Peggy McClelland

Afterward, the sightings and the sense that there's something else in the building, something not of this world, continued. The owners, however, have reached the conclusion that it is not the building that is haunted, but the personal items that were never buried with the deceased. Their hope is that once these items are out of the building, everything will be fine.

Meanwhile the couple has listed several items for sale on the eBay Web site, thinking that there probably is someone who would really like to have a piece of haunted history.

MARION COUNTY

❖❖❖❖❖❖❖❖❖ ORGANIZED IN 1822, the county was named for General Francis "Swamp Fox" Marion, an officer in the American Revolution. In the 1820s Alexander Ralston and Elias P. Fordham surveyed a site in central Indiana that had been suggested by the Conner Commission. Ralston, who assisted in laying out Washington, D.C., is probably most responsible for the plan of Indianapolis. A circle was placed in the middle of the capital, which was to be the center of the town's activities. Today it's the site of the Indiana Soldiers' and Sailors' Monument, dedicated in 1902.

By the 1830s Indianapolis was a major stopping point for the National Road traffic moving westward. Hopes for the Central Canal that would link the capital to the Wabash and Erie Canal were dropped after the depression of 1837. The only portion of that canal to be finished extended from the village of Broad Ripple to Indianapolis. The restoration of this section has become a destination for both tourists and citizens.

Indianapolis also became linked with the automobile industry in the early part of the last century. More than seventy different automobiles were manufactured in the capital, including the Cole, Duesenberg, Stutz, and Marmon. Today the automotive history is continued at the Indianapolis 500, the Brickyard 400, and the Formula One races. Indiana's capital city is a center of education, art, sports, manufacturing, and new biotech initiative industries. ❖

Hannah House

Hannah House, located at 3801 South Meridian, is a well known Indianapolis haunted house. The house was built in 1858 and is listed on the National Register of Historic Places; however, it's not the architecture that many are interested in, but its several ghosts.

The original owner of the house was Alexander Hannah, a birthright Quaker. He was believed to be a conductor on the Underground Railroad and used the cellar of this twenty-four-room mansion to hide fleeing slaves. This would later become the basis for some of the house's haunting legends.

One chilly evening, several runaway slaves—adults and children—arrived at the house. The frightened group, hungry and poorly clothed—some with only rags wrapped around their feet to ward off the cold—were welcomed into the Hannahs' home.

They were taken to the cellar to wait until arrangements could be made to safely send them to the next stop along the road to freedom. They were given fresh water, cold meats, and lanterns to illuminate the darkness of the tomb-like atmosphere. No one knows how it happened, but in the middle of the night a fire erupted! The trapped slaves panicked in their attempt to escape.

The screams and smell of burning flesh awakened the sleeping Hannah family and their servants. They rushed to put the fire out, but they were too late. Several from the group died that night. In order to protect the Hannah family and keep their secret as a stop on the Underground Railroad, it was necessary to bury the dead in shallow graves in the cellar where they had died.

The house was abandoned in the 1930s and sat empty until 1967 when its owner, David Elder, began restoring it. That is when the ghosts made themselves known.

Elder was the first to suspect the house was occupied. On a bleak, rain-soaked day in 1967, he was working alone in the house when he heard the sound of breaking glass in the cellar. He went to investigate, thinking kids had broken into the house and knocked over some old fruit jars. But he found nothing and no one—not even broken glass! Elder didn't say anything to anyone about the experience.

Later he hired a man to help with the renovations. The worker reported that he sometimes smelled something foul in one of the upstairs bedrooms, an odor he described as like that of decaying meat. At first Elder thought it might be a dead opossum or rat, but a thorough search was conducted and nothing was found.

The numerous experiences of hauntings at the Hannah House have drawn many investigators who have gone away convinced it truly is haunted. One of those investigators, a female psychic, was evidently unwilling to stay alone in the house, so she brought a friend with her. They stayed in the upstairs bedroom that had been reported to have a foul odor. After about fifteen minutes, they began hearing noises—eerie sounds of moaning and whining— and soon they both were overcome by a heavy sickening odor. The next day the owner took the women to the cellar, and there they swore they could smell sweat—like people packed closely together.

At one time, the Elders rented the house to an antique dealer and her husband. The woman's shop was on the first floor. She

Hannah House, once a stop on the Underground Railroad. PHOTO: Jonathan Tétreault

and her husband lived on the second. During the time they lived and worked there, they heard the inexplicable sound of breaking glass at least five times. Once they called the sheriff to investigate. He searched through the whole house, including the cellar, and found—nothing.

The antique dealer also experienced the sickening smell coming from a second floor bedroom. Thinking it was something that had permeated the old floorboards, she scrubbed the floor with carbolic acid, but the smell persisted. She decided to use the room only for storage and kept its door closed and locked. However, the door seemed to have a will of its own and would swing open out into the hallway. Once it was opened, an increase in other unexplained activities would occur—noises, footsteps, cold drafts, voices, and the opening and closing of other doors.

Others who have visited the house have reported seeing the apparition of a woman in one of the rooms and feeling a chill as the vision walked past. This female figure is believed to be the spirit of the Hannahs' German cook. But no one knows why she still stays in the house.

On another occasion, the antique dealer saw a man with mutton-chop whiskers wearing an old-fashioned black suit. He was seen walking across the upstairs hallway. At first she thought it was a customer who had wandered upstairs. By the time she reached the top of the stairs—he was gone.

When she told Elder of this experience, he produced a photograph of Alexander Hannah. The dealer was shocked! This was the image of the man she'd seen!

Later, she and her husband hired a painter to spruce up their living quarters. He, too, reported unusual occurrences such as doors swinging open and pictures falling from the walls. But perhaps the strangest occurrence happened when she brought him a cup of coffee on a tray with sugar, cream, and a teaspoon. As she sat the tray down on a table, the spoon suddenly flew across the room! The painter left the house and refused to return.

Her son offered to finish the painting in the evenings when he got off work. The first night he was there alone he felt very uncomfortable, as if he were being watched.

The next night he brought his wife and two young daughters with him. While painting he heard his youngest daughter, who was sitting on the stairs, talking to someone. When he went to investigate, he found only his daughter. Asking her who she had been talking to, she described a man in black. He ran up the stairs and encountered the man in black, who turned to him and said, "Get downstairs and take care of your own business."

These are but a few of the reported occurrences at Hannah House. Many strange things have happened in this house through the years—and probably still do.

House of Blue Lights

Another legendary house, one that no longer exists, was called the "House of Blue Lights." For many years stories were told about this house, which was located on a sixty-eight-acre wooded estate owned by an eccentric millionaire, Skiles Test. It was a strange house, partially constructed of glass block and white tile, with a huge glass swimming pool with underwater lights.

Stories say that Skiles's wife had died under mysterious circumstances. When she died, he refused to allow her body to be taken out of the house to be buried. He was deeply in love with her and could not bear to be without her. He had a glass coffin constructed. He dressed her in a blue formal gown, her favorite color, placed her in the coffin, and had it set upright in the living room. This room had three walls of picture windows. He chose that room as her final resting place so that she could look out on the surrounding woods. He then placed blue lights around the coffin and the room.

Next, he decorated the outside of the house and many of the trees in blue Christmas lights, and he put blue bulbs in the pool lights and in all of the flood lights throughout the grounds. Since the house was constructed with many glass blocks and tiles, it glowed eerily in the dark with the reflection of all those blue lights.

Local residents would drive by just to see the house glowing in the night. Some were even brave enough to go up to the house to see his wife—his sleeping beauty—in her glass coffin. They shared stories of seeing him sitting beside her, eating his evening meal and sipping wine. Some even reported that they thought they heard him talking to her. Others told of stumbling over several small tombstones as they crept up to the house. Some even said they had been shot at by the old man, and soon stories circulated about the many large, vicious dogs that ran wild through his estate.

Everybody who heard these stories wanted to see for themselves. They would drive to the location, and there on a slight rise they would see the glowing blue house. Some of these visitors even parked and would quietly walk through the open gates and up the drive. They, too, reported encountering the strange cemetery of many small tombstones. Some who ventured this far even said that in the stillness of the night, they had heard music. But then it would stop and become quiet—absolutely quiet. Suddenly, a shadow would begin moving toward them. They swore that it was the old man carrying a rifle. Then they would hear running feet and the snarling and barking of vicious dogs chasing after them as they ran for their lives.

The old man died in the late 1970s, and everything was sold at auction. He left the land to the Indianapolis Parks Department, and it became Skiles Test Park.

Thousands attended the estate sale to see his belongings and ask the auction's conductors about the stories—especially about the glass coffin containing his wife. They were told that there had been no glass coffin, no body in the house anywhere. But what about the cemetery with the many small tombstones? The explanation given was that it probably was a pet cemetery. The estate handlers further stated that nothing strange had ever happened at the estate, except for perhaps overactive imaginations and trespassing.

There are still many people who have heard the stories of the House of Blue Lights and just as many who swear to having gone there when Mr. Test was alive. If you ask them, they'll tell you what was "really" there.

Even today, some who have visited the park say the spirit of the house may still remain. They say that some nights, emanating from a slight rise—when everything is just right—you'll see an eerie blue glow.

MONTGOMERY COUNTY

❖❖❖❖❖❖❖❖❖❖THE COUNTY WAS orga-
nized in 1823 and named for Gen. Richard Montgomery,
a Revolutionary War officer who was killed in the Battle
of Quebec in 1775.

Montgomery County has one of Indiana's most beautiful and romantically rugged parks—Shades State Park.
The early name, The Shades of Death, eventually became
simply The Shades. Several stories account for how the
park acquired its name, but most emphasize that it was
named for the deep shadows of the forests in this area
when settlers arrived at this former Piankasaw Indian
settlement in the late 1820s. The 3,084-acre park was
established in 1947 primarily for hiking. The nearly eight
miles of trails—much of which cover steep cliffs and
rugged terrain—pass such romantic-sounding places as
Shawnee Canyon, Kickapoo Ravine, Lover's Leap, Devil's
Punch Bowl, and Maidenhair Falls. Sugar Creek cuts
through the park between high sandstone cliffs, creating
an outstanding vista from lookouts such as Prospect
Point (210 feet above the creek) and Lover's Leap.

Approximately five miles south of the park is Waveland.
Established in 1832 and named for a "gentleman's home
in Kentucky," this tiny town was the boyhood home of
artist T.C. Steele.

The county seat, Crawfordsville, was platted in 1823
by Major Ambrose Whitlock, who named it for Col.
William H. Crawford, a famous American Indian fighter
from Virginia who was secretary of war (1815–1816),
secretary of the treasury (1816–1825), and candidate for
the presidency in 1824 along with Andrew Jackson,
Henry Clay, and John Quincy Adams.

Crawfordsville is sometimes called the "Athens of Indiana" because of its cultural interests. It was one of the smallest cities in the country to have a symphony orchestra in the 1930s, and it has produced many fine artists, writers, educators, and politicians.

Local luminaries have included authors Lew Wallace, Meredith and Kenyon Nicholson, Will and Maurice Thompson, Caroline and Mary Hannah Krout, George Barr McCutcheon, Governor Henry Smith Lane, and "the father of the Indiana public school system," Caleb Mills (1806–1879). Both the Lew Wallace study and the Lane house are museums open to the public.

Crawfordsville's Old Jail Museum, located on North Washington Street, was built in 1882. It was the first of seven rotary jails constructed in the United States. The rotary cellblock consists of a two-tiered turntable divided into pie-shaped wedges, with a total of sixteen cells. The jailer would simply use a crank to rotate the mechanism to bring a particular cell to the opening, and in this way, prisoners would be moved in and out of the cells. The jail remained in use until 1967, although the rotating turn-table was immobilized in 1939. The jail was closed in 1973 and became a museum in 1975 operated by the Montgomery County Cultural Foundation.

Also located in Crawfordsville is Wabash College, a four-year private liberal arts school for men. Founded in 1832, it began as the Crawfordsville English and Classical High School. The school then became the Wabash Manual Labor College and Teachers' Seminary in 1834. In 1839 the name was shortened to Wabash College.

In 1833 Caleb Mills came to Crawfordsville from New Hampshire to teach the first class at Wabash College. For several years, Mills addressed the Indiana General Assembly at the start of its sessions urging them to establish a public school system in Indiana. Finally, in 1852, the new school system, providing a free education for every child in the state, went into operation. Mills became the second superintendent of public schools in 1854.

The R.R. Donnelley and Sons Company, located in Crawfordsville, is the nation's largest supplier of commercial printing services and is the city's leading industry since 1941, employing nearly two thousand people. ❖

The Devil's Creature

It happened on a crisp fall night in 1891. Two men were working at a local ice house on the outskirts of Crawfordsville when suddenly they both felt a presence. They weren't sure what it was, but it created a real sense of dread.

Looking toward the dark night sky, they saw what the local newspaper's account described as "a horrible apparition approaching from the west" three to four hundred feet in the air. According to the article, the witnesses estimated the creature's size as "eighteen feet long and eight feet wide." The mass moving through the air was pure white with a "flaming red eye." It made a strange "wheezing" and moaning sound much like a huge bellows.

Frozen to the spot, they continued to watch as it hovered directly over a house and then floated off to the east toward the city limits. Just as it reached the outskirts of Crawfordsville, it turned back to hover almost in the same location as it had before.

This strange story was not only reported in the local newspaper, but also in the September 5, 1891, issue of the *Indianapolis Journal*. At first many laughed at the story of these two men who had seen some kind of sky spirit, making jokes that they had probably consumed far too many liquid spirits.

However, another witness, one that could not be doubted, a Methodist minister, stepped forward stating that he and his wife had also witnessed the strange night vision. First they heard the strange wheezing and moaning sound. Going outdoors they saw what he described as a mass "about sixteen feet long and eight feet wide." Spellbound, they continued to observe the mass, which moved like a "serpent," rising up and down, circling the town, and then floating off.

Several Crawfordsville citizens watched the night sky hoping to get a glimpse of this strange creature. They were not disappointed. Two nights after the first sighting, several people from Craw-fordsville watched, stunned, as the red-eyed, wheezing, moaning, white mass dipped and rose above the city and then disappeared. This last sighting also was reported in Indiana papers as well as in the September 10, 1891, issue of the *Brooklyn Eagle.*

The citizens of Crawfordsville felt there was no doubt that what they had seen was one of the devil's creatures.

MORGAN COUNTY

❖❖❖❖❖❖❖❖❖❖ THE COUNTY, formed in 1821 and organized in 1822, was named for Brig. Gen. Daniel Morgan, who served under Benedict Arnold in Canada in 1775. The county is located on both sides of a glacial boundary. As a result, it is a study of geographical contrasts. The agriculturally rich soil in the northwest corner is the result of what had been a glacier. The glacier's termination is visible in the rocky and hilly southern region.

Straddling the border between Monroe and Morgan counties is the Morgan-Monroe Forest, the second largest forest in the state covering nearly twenty-four thousand acres.

The county seat, Martinsville, laid out in 1822 on an old Delaware trail, was named for one of its founders, John Martin. Martinsville was once known nationally as the "Artesian City" for its many mineral springs and health sanitariums. The springs were discovered in 1884 when a gas-drilling operation accidentally struck artesian water.

According to legend, the water's potential magical curing powers were not realized until an old racehorse that had been put out to pasture in the area drank the water and was revitalized. Once the word got out, health sanitariums began to spring up throughout the area, offering the curative powers of this elixir. The sanitarium era peaked during the first years of the twentieth century and significantly declined after about 1911.

From its beginning in 1899, the Home Lawn Sanitarium was the most famous of Martinsville's health spas and the last to close, in December 1973. The facility was built by Ebenezer Henderson, a Democratic party politician and friend of President Grover Cleveland. He visited the spa with his wife soon after its opening.

The elite and prestigious sanitarium hosted guests from the East Coast, Europe, England, and South Africa. Notable luminaries who visited the spa included entertainers Al Jolson, Mel Torme, and Phyllis Diller. Among the many politicians was the future President Franklin D. Roosevelt and Federal Bureau of Investigation Chief J. Edgar Hoover. Even the Beatles wanted to stay, but were turned away by the management who considered them to be too much of a security risk.

Samuel Moore came to the county in 1823, set up a general store, and began acquiring large tracts of land. The following year he laid out the town of Mooresville and attempted to establish a utopian community by giving free lots to those who shared similar educational and religious interests.

Mooresville is famous for being the home of Paul Hadley, designer of the Indiana State Flag. Another individual connected with Mooresville who captured national attention, was gangster John Dillinger. In 1920 the eighteen-year-old future gangster and his family moved from Indianapolis to a farm near Mooresville. Four years later he committed his first crime when he and another man attempted to rob a grocer at West Harrison and South Jefferson Streets. He was apprehended and sentenced to nine years in prison.

Waverly is the oldest existing village in Morgan County. It is noted for being the termination point of the pioneer Whetzel Trace, a sixty-mile path blazed through the Delaware Indian country in 1818 by Jacob Wetzel and his eighteen-year-old son Cyrus. The trail started at Laurel in Franklin County and, until 1827, was the route taken by most settlers who came from the east into central Indiana.
❖

Gravity Hill

Samuel Moore came to Morgan County from Salem, Indiana, in 1823. The following year the town of Mooresville was laid out and named for him. There Moore established a dry goods store, which, in 1828, became the town's first school. By 1831 Mooresville had a population of two hundred. Today there are more than ten thousand people living in the area. Many of these citizens, and others throughout the state and beyond, are familiar with the Gravity Hill mystery.

If you visit the area, you won't see a ghost, but that doesn't mean that you won't have a ghostly experience. Many who've come to the area swear they have.

It is said that if you pull your car to the bottom of Gravity Hill and put your car in neutral, it will slowly ascend the hill as if invisible hands are pushing it. And many say that's exactly what is happening.

There are several legends surrounding this location. One of these concerns a grandmother's love returning from beyond the grave. The woman lived in a house at the bottom of this hill. One day her grandson was playing in the middle of the road. The grandmother looked up and saw a car bearing down on the unsuspecting boy. She rushed into the roadway to grab him, but instead they were both hit and killed. Today, those who have experienced their car being pushed up the hill swear it is the grandmother and her grandson pushing.

This next legend is recounted as the truth behind the mystery of Gravity Hill. In the early days, when the American Indians made this area their home, there was a very important witch doctor. He was both admired and feared, for it was said he possessed a power far beyond the norm. It was also rumored he had amassed a great treasure of gold. He and his great treasure were buried at the foot of this hill.

Always fearful that someone will find his gold, the great energy and power he possessed in life still emanates from his grave and is used to keep his secret hidden. It is that power that he uses to move the cars on up the hill and away from his grave and gold.

If you're the type whose curiosity is piqued by life's mysteries, head for Mooresville and Gravity Hill. It won't be found on any map, but locals or the Mooresville Chamber of Commerce can direct you to the location if you're unable to find it using the following directions.

Starting in Mooresville, head west out of town on High Street (two blocks south of Main), which becomes State Road 42. Take the first right onto Keller Hill Road, and go approximately one mile over a few small hills. Stop when you come to what is referred to as the "big hill."

Now, put your car in neutral and you, too, may experience the mystery of Gravity Hill.

PUTNAM COUNTY

❖❖❖❖❖❖❖❖❖❖ NAMED FOR Gen. Israel Putnam, an officer in the American Revolution, Putnam County was formed in 1821 and organized the following year. In 1823, the county seat was established on land that had been donated for that purpose by Ephraim Dukes. It was called Greencastle. One local legend says the name came from the first man who settled in this area. As the story goes, he built his home on a log foundation, and after the house was built the logs sprouted and began to grow—so he called it his green castle. While that story is still told in Putnam County today, it is now known that the city was named for Greencastle, Pennsylvania, the hometown of the earliest settler.

A plaque located at the southwest corner of Washington and Indiana Streets commemorates the site of one of the town's first buildings: Eli Lilly's first drugstore. In 1852, the Lilly family moved to Greencastle, where Eli attended preparatory school at Indiana Asbury College (present-day DePauw University).

Also notorious in the town was the Central National Bank of Greencastle, originally located on the southwest corner of the courthouse square. The bank was robbed by the infamous John Dillinger gang on October 23, 1933, and the gang made away with $75,000, which is believed to be the largest amount the gang ever stole in a single robbery.

Two of the county's oldest institutions, which provide continuing stability to its economy, are the Indiana State Farm, founded as a penal farm in 1821, and DePauw University, founded in 1837 as Asbury College. Founded by the Methodist church, Asbury labored under financial difficulties when, on the brink of closing, Washington

Charles DePauw came to its rescue in the 1880s. It was renamed DePauw in honor of its benefactor in 1884.

With nine remaining covered bridges, Putnam County is second in the state only to Parke County, which boasts thirty-two existing bridges and is considered the "covered bridge capital of the world." Originally Putnam County had thirty known covered bridges in addition to two it shared with neighboring counties. ✤

Edna Collins Bridge

One of Putnam County's nine remaining covered bridges is the Edna Collins Bridge, built in 1922 across Little Walnut Creek on County Route 450, one mile northwest of Clinton Falls. Ironically, it was built to replace a concrete bridge washed out by high waters.

Reputed to be haunted, the bridge is steeped in mystery: Who really built the bridge? Was there an Edna Collins? If so, is she the one who haunts the bridge? Many say that there are actually two ghosts haunting the bridge. There are several stories and theories concerning all of these questions.

The Edna Collins Bridge is considered the "baby" of all Indiana bridges. It is the state's only covered bridge that was built in the twentieth century. Some records indicate the builder was either George Collins or Collings, while others list the builder as George Hendricks or Hendrix.

Susan Harmon, a Putnam County librarian, did an exhaustive search to try and solve this mystery, but to no avail. There was a family of Collins/Collings in the area at the time the bridge was built, but no George. She had much the same problem locating any information on a George Hendricks/Hendrix. One thing seems to be certain: The Edna Collins bridge was built by a George.

But was there an Edna connected with the Collins/Collings family? Apparently, yes. She was the daughter of James and Sarah

Newgent Collings, who were married in Putnam County on August 17, 1837.

In the 1860 census Sarah was listed as a forty-six-year-old widow with four children: John, twenty; Wm. G., eighteen; Nancy, fifteen; and Edna, ten. The last time Edna appears in the census records was in 1920. At that time she was listed as single head of house, age sixty-eight. Two years later the Edna Collins covered bridge was built and christened in her name.

For several decades stories have been told about the ghosts of Edna Collins bridge. The legend begins in the early 1920s when a little girl drowned in Little Walnut Creek just beneath the bridge.

Her parents often traveled into Greencastle. The little girl would beg to be allowed to stay behind with her dog and swim in Little Walnut Creek. Often her parents would agree and drop her off along the way. They wouldn't be gone long, and she was to listen for the car horn that would signal their return.

On one of these occasions, when the parents returned to the bridge her father honked, but she did not come. Thinking she hadn't heard the first time, he honked again, and they waited. She still didn't appear. He honked a third time. When they didn't get a response, her parents got out of the car to look for her.

There on the bank sat her dog, soaked. He ran to them, jumping and running back to the water's edge. He continued until the girl's parents reached the bank. There in the middle of the creek lay their daughter, facedown in the water. Her father rushed into the water, the distraught pet bounding after him. Once back on the bank her father tried unsuccessfully to breathe life into his little girl.

Since that horrible day the ghost of the little girl is said to haunt the bridge. Throughout the years, many people who have heard this story have visited the bridge and have seen the little girl they call Edna Collins for lack of another name. Some say they've seen her standing at the end of the bridge with her dog beside her, waiting.

There might be another young girl haunting this bridge, however. The story begins in the mid-1800s at the village of Portland

Mills, not too far from Clinton Falls. According to folklore, there was a doctor from Clinton Falls who was seeing a young girl from the community, and he had gotten her pregnant. He performed an unsuccessful abortion. The young girl died. For several years this story circulated along with sightings of a girl at the Portland Mills covered bridge.

Portland Mills no longer exists. In 1896 it became part of the lake bottom of the Cecil B. Harden Lake at Raccoon State Recreation Area, and the Portland Mills covered bridge was relocated to Little Raccoon Creek in Parke County.

Some of the former citizens of Portland Mills believe the young girl's ghost wanted to stay in Putnam County, where she lived and died. They believe she has taken up residence at the Edna Collins Bridge. Thus, the town of Portland Mills is no more—but its spirit lives on.

Edna Collins covered bridge, near Clinton Falls. PHOTO: Ruth Holladay

RANDOLPH COUNTY

❖❖❖❖❖❖❖❖❖ THIS COUNTY was organized in 1818. The derivation of its name remains a mystery. It may have been named for Randolph County, North Carolina, the home of many early pioneers; or it may have been named for Thomas Randolph (1771–1811), who was attorney general for Territorial Governor William Henry Harrison; or for Thomas Mann Randolph (1768–1828), Virginia statesman, who was Thomas Jefferson's son-in-law. In the same year the county was founded, Winchester was chosen as the county seat. Like the county's name, Winchester's name has more than one possible source. It may have been named for an English town, or chosen to honor Brig. Gen. James Winchester, an officer in the War of 1812.

Although the county is generally flat, it has the highest average elevation of Indiana's counties. This accounts for Randolph County being the headwater region for several major rivers including the Mississinewa, the West Fork of Whitewater, and the West Fork of White rivers. A journalist once wrote that the county was the "mother of rivers."

Winchester was the home of the Winchester Speedway, considered to be the world's fastest half-mile track—that is, it has the fastest qualifying time of any half-mile track. Established in 1914 by Frank Funk, it is the state's second oldest racetrack. However, the track was forced to suspend operation for the 2004 season due to financial difficulties. Midway through that season, the future of the track remained uncertain: The owners still have not announced whether their plans are to re-open the speedway or to place it for sale. The closing of this track came as a great shock to the racing industry.

On the northeast corner of Winchester's courthouse lawn stands a sixty-seven-foot-high Civil War Monument. Completed in 1892, this is the second in size only to the Soldiers' and Sailors' Monument in Indianapolis. A.A. McKain of Indianapolis designed the oolitic limestone and Vermont granite monument. It originally was to be topped by a status of the war god, Mars; however, it was replaced by a more suitable figure of an American soldier. The lower section depicts a fort with sixteen canons. Above the fort are four figures, each six feet high, representing the four branches of military service—infantry, artillery, cavalry, and navy. These figures were sculpted by the famous artist, Lorado Taft (1860–1936).

Winchester was the home of the colorful James E. Watson, known as "Sunny Jim." He was a U.S. representative and Indiana senator for twenty-eight years between 1895 and 1933. He lived in Winchester until age twenty-nine, when he moved to Rushville.

Union City is one of those unique border towns. Half in Indiana and half in Ohio, the city is divided by a street. Union City was platted in Ohio in 1838 and in Indiana in 1849. The location of this city in both states may have in-fluenced the name. The Indiana and Ohio sections remain separate corporations with their own governments, tax rates, police schools, firehouses, water systems, and even two time zones during part of the year; however, the Federal government recognized Union City as a unified city by establishing a single post office.

Union City was the home of Indiana governor, Isaac P. Gray (1825–1895). After the Civil War, Gray established the Citizens State Bank in Union City, and subsequently served as a state senator (1869–1871), lieutenant governor (1877–1880), acting governor (1880–1881), governor (1885–1889), and minister to Mexico (1893–1895). ❖

The Ghost House

Can a house have a spirit? Can that spirit survive after the house is destroyed? One man believes it is possible. His name has been lost, but not the story. He was living in Richmond while completing his architectural studies at Ball State University in 1989. He commuted using *u.s.* Route 35, and each day, just after he'd pass through the little town of Economy and enter Randolph County, he'd see the remains of an old farm. The house was gone. All that was left was a sagging barn and a group of trees where the house had been.

Everyday he passed this abandoned and forlorn farm and wondered about the house. Who had lived there? What had happened to the house? Had it been torn down? Or had it burned?

After graduation he returned to his hometown in northern Indiana. In the spring of 1991, he was going to Columbus, Ohio, for a job interview. He wanted to stop at Ball State to get a transcript of his grades and decided to once again drive past the old farm on his way into Ohio.

When he reached the farm, he saw that someone had built a house where the original farmhouse had once stood. It was after eight o'clock in the evening and he could see the lights shining in the windows.

The house had a simple rectangular style, with two windows on either side of the front door and five windows across the front of the second floor. He thought to himself that this was probably very much like the original farmhouse.

He left Columbus the following Sunday afternoon, and even though it was a little out of his way, he decided to drive back past the farm and get a better look at the house.

He drove through Economy. Within a few miles he came upon the site of the old farm. As he drove past he couldn't believe what he was seeing—or what he wasn't seeing.

There was no house! All that was there was the old barn and the group of trees. But he knew he'd seen a house lit up that night on his way to Ohio.

What explanation could there be? Those who believe in or have experienced the presence of ghosts feel that if people experience traumatic deaths, their spirits are destined forever to stay in that place where they died. Could the spirit of a house that had been destroyed by perhaps by some tragic means still exist? There is at least one man who believes this is possible.

SHELBY COUNTY

❖❖❖❖❖❖❖❖❖❖ THIS COUNTY was formed in 1821 and named for Isaac Shelby, an officer in both the Revolutionary War and the War of 1812, and the first governor of Kentucky (1792–1796 and 1812–1816). The county is agriculturally diverse, but corn is king—with soybeans a close second.

Shelbyville, the county seat, was platted in 1822 and named for the county. More than half of the land donated for the establishment of the county seat came from John Hendricks. His son, Thomas A. Hendricks, was the unsuccessful Democratic running mate of Samuel Tilden in 1876 and became Vice President under Grover Cleveland in 1885. Unfortunately, Thomas Hendricks died less than nine months after his inauguration.

Located a short distance from the entrance of the Shelby County Fairgrounds is the Thomas Hendricks log cabin. Hendricks was born in Zanesville, Ohio, in 1819. The family moved to Shelbyville when he was three. The cabin was reconstructed in 1962 from many of the logs of the first cabin built by his father, John, on the east edge of Shelbyville near the point where Michigan Road crosses Little Blue River.

Another of Shelbyville's famous sons was Charles Major (1856–1913), a Shelbyville lawyer and author. His first book, *When Knighthood Was in Flower*, was published in 1898. But perhaps he's best known for his adventure story, *The Bears of Blue River*, which had a local setting.

Shelbyville's Thomas A. Hendricks Grade School and Charles Major Memorial School give testament to the community's pride in and honor of these two men.

Another citizen of Shelbyville who has received national

recognition is Sandy Allen. At seven-feet-seven-inches, the *Guinness Book of World Records* considers her to be the world's tallest woman.

Shelbyville was the site of Indiana's first railroad. Near the intersection of Broadway and Harrison Streets is a historical marker recognizing Judge William J. Peasley's short-lived experimental railroad, which began operation on July 4, 1834. The horse-drawn wooden cars carried passengers over wooden rails for one and one-quarter miles from the east side of Shelbyville to a picnic area on Lewis Creek.

Highlighting the Shelbyville Public Square are two notable works of art. The Joseph Memorial Fountain designed in 1923 by George H. Honig (1874–1962), a Rockport, Indiana, native. Honig's design depicts a group sculpture of three youths holding various implements of summer fun. The work was financed by a $5,000 legacy of German immigrant Julius Joseph. At the time of his death in 1920 he requested that the money be used to erect a city fountain on the square.

The second notable work of art was executed by Mary Elizabeth Stout in 1929 and is an Italian-cast bronze statue depicting Major's *Bears of Blue River* saga. The sculpture features Balsar Brent, the novel's hero, holding his two pet bear cubs, Tom and Jerry. Originally the statue was placed at the entrance to the nearby Charles Major Elementary School until it was moved to the present location in 1980.

Morristown, a short distance from Shelbyville, was platted in 1828 and named for one of the founders, Samuel Morrison. Of significant note is the Kopper Kettle Restaurant located on U.S. Route 52. Originally built as a grain elevator in the late 1840s, it was abandoned when the Junction Railroad was discontinued. It was later purchased and converted into the Old Davis Tavern and Hotel in 1858. The same family has owned and operated the building since

1860. From 1885 to 1923 the restaurant and hotel went by the name of the Valley House. At the later date, the hotel section was abandoned, and the name was changed to the Kopper Kettle. Among some of the famous who have dined in this historic building are James Whitcomb Riley, Henry Ford, Wendell Willkie, Herbert Hoover, and Charles Lindbergh. Although many exterior and interior changes have taken place over the years, a visit to the restaurant is still considered a premier family dining experience. ❖

The Blue River Concert

Shelby County had a real music lover, according to legend. He was a musician. His instrument of choice was the organ.

The man, a farmer, lived near Shelbyville along the Blue River. Everyday when his chores were done he'd sit at his organ and play for hours. Or at least as long as his wife could stand it.

His wife did not enjoy the organ music. Finally she told him if he wanted to play the organ to put it in the barn where she would not have to hear the noise. Obediently, the farmer moved his beloved organ to the barn. After supper he'd go to the barn and play for hours into the night.

Everyone in the area at the time knew this story. And many driving past the house late at night would tell of hearing the strange sound of organ music coming from the barn.

Both the husband and wife are now deceased. For many years their house has stood empty. Yet on moonlit nights the old house and barn take on an eerie and ghostly appearance. Teenagers in and around the Shelbyville area soon found these forlorn buildings, and the spooky site became a perfect place to take a date.

While driving to the farm, the teens would tell stories of hauntings, ghosts floating about the countryside, and other strange and frightening happenings. By the time the teenaged couple arrived, it was not too farfetched to believe the old farm was haunted.

Several couples who visited the Blue River site came away convinced that it truly was haunted. Stories were told of hearing ghostly strains of organ music wafting across the night air.

No one knows—or will tell—exactly the location of the farm. Is the old farmer still playing his haunting Blue River concert?

The Enchanted Sisters

An old favorite Shelby County pioneer legend tells the story of three enchanted sisters.

It was a time when hunters and trappers blazed their own trails. Wild game was plentiful in the dense and dark forests. The area was sparsely inhabited and log cabins were few and far between. People knew very little about their nearest neighbors since they lived several miles apart.

The early pioneers in the area listened to the tales told by trappers and hunters of their encounters with three beautiful, mysterious, and reclusive sisters living alone in a log cabin deep in the forest. Superstition pronounced them to be either fairies or witches.

The gamesmen, fearless in their meetings with wild animals and Indians, could not bring themselves to approach the three beauties. Hiding behind tree, they'd watch the lithe figures leave their home and stroll into the dense woods where they'd change into wild animals. As the three left the woods to return to their log cabin, they'd quickly change back into the images of the three beautiful sisters.

There was one hunter in the area well known for his ability to track and kill deer. He took great pride in telling of his exploits in deer hunting. The season of the deer was approaching. With great care the man prepared himself and his weapons. The time for hunting was at hand.

Venturing deep into the forest in an unfamiliar area, he hoped to find plenty of deer. After some time he came upon three deer.

Very quietly he approached them, and positioning himself to take careful aim, he fired. The three deer scampered away unscathed. The hunter was surprised. He had had a clear shot. Something must have been wrong with his gun.

Returning to his cabin, he carefully went over the gun and found nothing wrong. He then set up a target to see if something could be wrong with the sight. Everything checked out.

The next day he went back to where he'd first seen the three deer. After several hours he found them standing in a shaft of sunlight. Slowly and quietly he was able to get close to them. Taking careful aim, he shot. And again, he apparently missed.

The next day he went to town. Arriving at the trader's store, he was greeted by the other men swapping hunting tales. When asked how many deer he'd killed, he replied that he hadn't killed any thus far. The other men knowing of his boastful hunting stories began ribbing him.

He then told them of the strange events. The men offered numerous suggestions as to what could've happened. An old hunter listening quietly walked over to the group and told the hunter he had the same experience many years ago. It was his belief that these deer were enchanted. The hunter was advised to melt some silver coins and mold them into bullets, with which he would be able to kill them.

He did as the old man suggested. As soon as the task was completed he set out once more in search of the three. Just as the sun was coming up he saw them running and scampering about. Taking careful aim, he shot at one of them just as it jumped to one side. It was wounded.

The other two immediately darted off and disappeared. The hunter was able to follow the wounded and slower deer. Soon a log cabin came into view. The deer headed straight for it. Just as it neared the door, it disappeared.

The hunter watched in wonderment as he saw the form of a young girl appear where the deer had stood. As she entered the cabin, the hunter noticed she was limping. Cautiously, he approached the ca-bin. Standing in the open doorway, he saw two very beautiful young ladies standing by a bed. Lying on the bed was another beautiful young girl, one of her feet bleeding.

The two girls turned, startled by the man's voice. In amazement he said, "You three sisters appeared as deer in the woods, and I shot the one lying on the bed and trailed her to the cabin."

The three sisters acknowledged that this was true. They begged him not to divulge their hiding place. He agreed, and after apologizing and making sure the wounded sister would recover, he left the cabin.

Although the hunter heard others talk about the legend of the three enchanted sisters, he never divulged their hiding place. Nor did he ever tell of his encounter. Who would've believed him in any event?

UNION COUNTY

✤✤✤✤✤✤✤✤✤ UNION, INDIANA'S second smallest county, was organized in 1821. The name is believed to have been chosen to suggest harmony and patriotism.

Standing on the southeast side of the courthouse lawn is the Templeton Cabin, the oldest surviving log structure in the county. The cabin was originally built in 1804, a few miles south of Dunlapsville. It was moved to Liberty in 1838 as a memorial to John Templeton (1766–1837), the cabin's builder who had served in the Territorial General Assembly in 1810 and 1811.

The county seat, Liberty, was laid out the following year. Liberty was the home of Maj. Gen. Ambrose E. Burnside (1824–1881). Burnside's father, a state senator, obtained a West Point appointment for his son in 1843. During the Civil War, Burnside's son briefly commanded the Army of the Potomac. It is well known that Burnside sported magni-ficent side whiskers—ever after referred to as "sideburns."

Union County's Treaty Line Museum is a pioneer village grouping of restored log cabins and other structures. The county is also home to the Sixteenth State Park, Whitewater Memorial State Park. The 1,710-acre park was dedicated in 1949 as a living memorial to the men and women who served in World War II. ✤

The Spirit of Hanna House

In the September-October 2003 issue of the *Whitewater Valley Explorer* there appeared a story about an old brick home near Dunlapsville. Not just any home, this is a haunted home.

Everyone who has owned the house has added to it to meet their needs. Some intended to make it a commercial venture. For others, it served as a restaurant. The most recent owners, Mark and Cheryl Stolle, wanted to restore the house as their home. The old home has had nearly two-dozen owners before the Stolles.

The two-story brick home at 3130 South Old Dunlapsville Road was built on property granted to Capt. John Hanna by the u.s. government in 1804. It took the government ten years before the land deed was finally issued in 1814.

The Stolles purchased the home from Steven J. Leonard, who had intended to tear down some architectural features and then remake the house into a bed and breakfast. He'd gotten as far as the tearing down. Floors, walls, and staircases were missing. To enter the second floor, the Stolles had to prop a ladder against the side of the house, climb in through a window, and step out onto an area with no sub flooring.

Family members thought the Stolles had lost their mind. The house was more than a hundred years old—the spirit waiting. The charm of the house had reached out to them and the Stolles believed they could make this a home. It felt right, like destiny, like they'd been chosen.

Union County folk, however, believed the house to be haunted, and told stories of seeing a ghostly female apparition in the house. Named Jenny, she appears to be a wistful young woman in a long dress.

In the course of the Stolles' renovation, Mark Stolle took several before-and-after pictures throughout the house, including in the upper bedroom, which is reputed to have been Jenny's. In every developed picture, there's a washed-out area in the images taken in this room. Mark moved all around in the room to achieve different camera angles for his pictorial record. But, on the developed photographs, from every angle, the washed-out area doesn't move! It's seemingly rooted in the same spot no matter where in the room the camera was aimed.

The pictures where the spot appears come from the middle of the roll, not the beginning or the end where an overexposure is more likely to have occurred. What could have created this phenomenon? Could Mark have photographed the wistful image of Jenny?

Since the Stolles moved in, they haven't seen Jenny or any of the house's other prior residents. The family feels that Jenny must approve of the changes made by the current owners and that she is apparently quite content.

The Tilted Mill

In December 1911, the *Liberty Herald* reprinted an article written by T.L. Dickerson in 1905 titled "The Tilted Mill" that recounted the remarkable mystery of an old grist mill having been turned around and moved from its foundation while the proprietor and his family slept.

The strange, but allegedly true, incident took place in 1845 during the early Union County pioneer days at the Brown Mill located on the East Whitewater River on land owned by Henry Masters. The mill owner, Peter Rudman, operated both a wool and grain mill with the same water power and turbine wheel.

On the day before the strange occurrence, the sun shone bright and warm, birds were flitting about, the sky was clear, and there were no indications of storms or tornados. With such good weather, many wagons from up and down the valley were lined up with sacks of corn and wheat to be ground.

Rudman was unable to accommodate that many customers in one day. A number of them had to leave their bags and return the next day for their flour.

The miller worked all day and continued grinding until nearly midnight. Before going to bed, he gave orders to his son, John, to get up early the next morning and turn on the water from the head gates so he could get an early start on the next day's grinding.

At dawn John went down to the mill. He came running back white as a ghost, eyes bulging, frightened out of his wits, stuttering, and stammering. He told his mother he couldn't enter the mill. It had turned partially around on its foundation!

She couldn't believe what her son had told her. How could a mill turn on its foundation? She hastened to awaken her husband. After hearing this unbelievable story, he hurriedly dressed and went down to the mill to see for himself. Arriving, he could not believe his eyes! Was this a dream? He was totally mystified. He returned to the house completely dumbfounded.

Peter Rudman and his family were frightened beyond belief. This must be a warning from some mysterious power. The devil? A witch? They began to believe that attempting to enter the mill would mean certain death.

Why had this happened to the good-hearted, hard-working miller and his family? Although the family was God-fearing—they prayed and read the Bible every evening before retiring—the Rudmans also believed, as many of the early pioneers did, that you must never ignore or tamper with the uncanny powers of evil spirits, ghosts, or witches. Therefore, before he ever began milling, Rudman had taken the precaution of nailing a horse shoe above the door. He had also melted a silver coin and molded it into a bullet, which he placed in his rifle and fired into the air in an effort to scare off evil spirits. What had gone wrong?

The news of this phenomenon soon spread like a great wave across the valley and beyond. The curious from the surrounding countryside came to view this great mystery. They came from as far away as Brookville, Harrison, and Lawrenceburg, and as eastward as Oxford and Hamilton, Ohio. They came from Connersville, Cam-bridge City, Laurel, and Liberty, and as far north as Richmond.

From actual measurements, the mill had turned more than seven feet on its original foundation! How could mere mortals put right what magic had done? How could they move a two-story brick structure back into its original position?

Adam Pigman, a carpenter, suggested that if enough force could be obtained the mill could be moved back by the use of lever power and brute strength. Although the Rudmans were still fearful, they knew something had to be done and felt they'd be safe with all their friends around them.

They chose a day to try and move the mill back on its foundation. Everybody for miles around was requested to come with axes, log chains, crosscut saws, and teams. Wives and sweethearts were to bring well-filled baskets. Peter Rudman, feeling less fearful, put out the word that he'd furnish a barrel of sparkling cider on the designated day.

Men with teams were given the task of cutting and hauling long poles, trees, and saplings, to be used as levers. Others brought hand spikes. Meanwhile, the blacksmith had made iron ends to place on the pike poles or levers. The women supplying the men with food had their work cut out for them.

More than 160 men and boys came to the mill on the designated day. Many, including the Rudman family, still felt this had been the work of a supernatural power, probably a witch. Before the task to turn and right the mill began, the minister led the gathering in prayer, requesting a blessed intervention to right this "queer business" and to bless all those who were there that day and their efforts.

Taking their positions on opposite sides of the mill, the men began working with the levers on a fulcrum, straining their muscles. The first attempt moved the mill six inches. The effort continued throughout the day until the mill was finally turned back into place on its foundation!

For many years, the miller continued his work with no other strange or uncanny happenings. The mystery of the tilted mill was never solved.

SOUTHERN
INDIANA

DAVIESS COUNTY

❖❖❖❖❖❖❖❖❖ DAVIESS County was founded in 1816 and named for Capt. Joseph Hamilton Daviess, who was killed leading a charge at the Battle of Tippecanoe (1811). The county is rich in natural resources such as coal, iron ore, sandstone, and limestone. However, much of the county is agricultural. A large Amish settlement farms the area northwest of Loogootee.

Washington, the county seat, began on the site of Fort Flora, a timber fort erected by David Flora in 1812. Today the fort would be located on Main and Second Streets. In 1815, Flora, Isaac Galland, and George Curtis laid out the town of Liverpool, incorporating the fort. When the county commissioners chose Liverpool to be the county seat in 1817, its name was changed to Washington to reflect its location in Washington Township.

The small town of Odon was originally laid out as Clarksburg in 1846. A post office was established there in 1856 at Perkins Store; in 1857 it was changed to Walnut Hill. One year later it was renamed Clarks Prairie. Finally, in 1881, the name was changed to Odon. It is believed that the town's name was inspired by the Norse god, Odin; however, the folklore story regarding the town's name does not have anything to do with a Norse god.

According to tradition, the townspeople expected the town to become a second Terre Haute and wanted a more progressive-sounding name. In the winter of 1881, a group of men sat around the stove in the post office in hot debate on what the new name would be. "Garfield" was proposed, after the newly-elected president. Finally it was decided to name the town after the two loudest agitators for the name change, Joe Dun Laughlin and Caleb O'Dell. "O" for O'Dell and "don" for Joe Dun. ❖

The Odon Fires

Throughout history there have been several cases of mysterious fires erupting without the aid of human hands or by accident of nature. What causes spontaneous immolations? In an effort to explain this phenomenon, some have theorized that ghosts, specifically poltergeists, could be the cause of these mysterious events.

The William Hackler family near Odon, Indiana, experienced this peculiar phenomenon. It began early one morning in April 1941. The family had finished breakfast when one of the family members smelled smoke.

The Hacklers began searching throughout the house for the source. Soon a small blaze was found just below the window in a seldom-used second-floor bedroom. The fire seemed to be coming from within the wall!

The Odon Volunteer Fire Department responded. The fire was quickly extinguished.

What was strange about this fire was the fact that the house had no electricity! No member of the family could've set the fire inside the wall. In any event, they were all in the kitchen at the time they first smelled the smoke.

The fire department returned to Odon only to be called back to the Hackler farm, where in another bedroom Mrs. Hackler discovered the mattress smoldering. This fire, too, appeared to be burning from within.

Fires began spontaneously erupting throughout the house. Be-tween eight o'clock and eleven o'clock that morning, nine fires were extinguished. An Odon volunteer fireman noticed a thin wisp of smoke coming from a bookshelf in the living room. He picked up one of the books and discovered a small fire beginning to burn inside the book's covers. Even a pair of Mr. Hackler's overalls hanging behind a door went up in flames. A calendar hanging on the kitchen wall also ignited. While neighbors watched in amazement, a bedspread hanging on the clothesline turned to ashes.

The fires continued throughout the day. No room in the house was spared, and yet nothing of great value was seriously damaged. Observers noted only small things, such as clothing and household items, exploded into flame. The house itself, with the exception of the first fire in the wall, never caught flame! It was as if an invisible hand was lighting invisible matches.

The Odon Volunteer Fire Department was joined by other volunteer firefighters from two nearby communities. At day's end the firefighters had extinguished a total of twenty-eight fires!

The family was fearful of spending the night in the house. They moved their beds outside and spent the night beneath the stars. The next day neighbors offered them a place to stay until they felt safe returning to their home. They never did return.

A week later Mr. Hackler dismantled the house, and using the lumber, built another home several miles away. The family was never again plagued with mysterious fires.

Reporters and fire investigators attempted to explain how these fires could have happened. Officials closed the case, describing it as a "most baffling mystery."

According to stories circulating in the community, the Traveler's Insurance Company later published a full-page advertisement in an edition of Collier's Magazine describing the Hacklers' fires. Presumably the company had insured the family against loss by fire—any kind of fire!

DECATUR COUNTY

❖❖❖❖❖❖❖❖❖ ORGANIZED IN 1821, the county was named for Com. Stephen Decatur, naval hero of the 1812 conflict with England. The county seat, Greensburg, was founded in 1820 by Col. Thomas Hendricks, brother of an Indiana governor and uncle to a U.S. Vice President. The town was named for Greensburg, Pennsylvania, the home of Hendricks's wife.

Notable Hoosier writers Edward and George Eggleston lived a few years of their youth in Decatur County during the early 1850s. A cloak-and-dagger episode in the Milford area was the basis of the plot in Edward's *The Hoosier Schoolmaster* (1871). George's novel *Jack Shelby* (1906) also drew on Decatur County experiences and individuals.

The town of Greensburg is perhaps best known for its live trees growing on the courthouse tower. The "tower trees" have delighted observers for more than a century. Theories abound about why the trees are able to survive in such a precarious location. They've been identified as members of the large-tooth Aspen family, and this fact gave rise to a local columnist's comment that the trees' tenacity "was based on their ability to hang on by the skin of their big teeth."

Greensburg is also the birthplace of Carl G. Fisher (1874–1939). Although Fisher left school after the sixth grade, he went on to help found the Indianapolis Motor Speedway, develop Miami beach, and influence the building of two highways—the Lincoln and the Dixie.

Wilbur Shaw (1902–1954), a three-time winner of the Indianapolis 500 and Speedway president, also spent a portion of his youth in Greensburg.

B.B. Harris, a scout for Morgan's Raiders, passed through the Greensburg area and, after the Civil War, returned in 1869 to found the village of Harris City, five miles south of Greensburg. He opened a large limestone quarry, which provided stone for the Indiana Statehouse, Cincinnati's U.S. Customhouse, and other buildings.

Brig. Gen. John T. Wilder, leader of the famed "Lightning Brigade," also made his home in Greensburg after the Civil War. Wilder's brigade often chased Confederate raiders. He also is known for arming his men with Spencer repeating rifles, thus making his brigade the first Civil War unit to be armed with Spencers.

His brick-and-stone home, Wildwood, is located in Greensburg at 446 East Main Street. Shortly after its construction, he moved to Chattanooga, Tennessee, serving a term as its mayor. He died there in 1917. ❖

The Friendly Ghost

On two occasions, Pat Smith, columnist for the *Greensburg Daily News,* wrote about one man's encounter with a friendly ghost. Ac-cording to the story in her columns, four generations of one Greens-burg family have passed on this haunting tale as part of their family lore. Today it's become part of Hoosier folklore. It is the account of one family member's experience with a friendly ghost.

Charles H. Oliger was born in Decatur County in 1884. Long before his death in 1930, he told his son-in-law, John Thrine, of his amazing encounter with a friendly ghost.

When Charles was a young man in the early 1900s, he lived with his parents on South East Street near the entrance to South Park Cemetery. One evening he walked uptown to spend time with some of his friends. As night fell, he said goodbye and began his walk home. Nearing the stone bridge over Gas Creek, he saw a tall man walking toward him. Charles noticed that the man was dressed in formal attire—a high silk hat and tails.

As they met on the bridge, the young man said, "Good evening," to the dignified stranger. The gentleman politely tipped his hat and walked on. Somewhat intrigued at meeting someone at that time of the evening and in formal attire, the young man turned to take another look. There was no one in sight!

Had this really happened, or had it been his imagination? He decided to keep the experience to himself, at least for a while. He and his "imagination" did meet at the bridge at least once more. Again the distinguished specter politely tipped his hat and disappeared at the end of the bridge. The young man decided to share this strange experience and discovered several others had also met the mysterious phantom.

One of the buildings that the young Charles passed on his walk home was the South Park Monument Company located at 318 South East Street. Could the apparition have been someone connected with this business? An undertaker from the past?

The encounters at the bridge were not forgotten, but were disregarded for several years as Charles matured, married, and started his own business. After World War II, he purchased the monument company building and opened the Oliger Paint & Wallpaper Store, where he and his sons worked for many years. If the spirit he had encountered at the bridge was connected to the monument building, Charles either didn't experience anything in the building or didn't tell anyone.

Although Charles remained skeptical about the existence of the ghost, he knew that he had seen something that couldn't be ex-plained.

Today the Scheidler Brothers Decorating store occupies the old monument building. They have felt a presence upstairs in the building. Is it the phantom of the bridge?

Greensburg Courthouse Ghost

There's a ghost in the basement of the Greensburg Courthouse. Well, some say there is, while others say there isn't. But certainly strange and unexplained things have happened. *Greensburg Daily News* columnist Pat Smith interviewed a number of courthouse employees about the ghost for her October 28, 1998, article.

She writes of the ghost: "He never appeared in the traditional white drapes, nor did he yell, 'Booooo!' at anyone in all the years." She further states that many have "experienced his presence and just as many won't talk about it."

The meetings with the ghost usually take place when employees need to work late at night. The haunting isn't something they can put their finger on. Mostly the workers feel his presence pass them in the hallways. The air changes. It's like a breeze that is created when someone quickly walks by.

There have also been a few reports of people feeling a gentle touch or tap—and yet there wasn't anyone near. Those who have had this experience state they felt the hair on the back of their neck and arms stand at attention.

One courthouse worker Smith interviewed offers this account of his encounters with the ghost: "I've heard a pecking noise and it's not a pipe or a bird. An ashtray was moved one time when there was

Greensburg County Courthouse. PHOTO: Pat Smith

absolutely no one else around. When I was making copies one time, the door kept closing. It did that three times and finally I said, 'Look, ghost! Leave me alone.' And it did."

Another employee also cites the experience of running copies in the basement and feeling strongly that someone, or something, was watching either from the stairs or from under the stairway. There was no other human near the copier.

Apparently, a couple of people have even brought their dogs to the courthouse when they had to work late, and while they didn't hear or feel anything, the dogs certainly did. They became very alert and even bristled as if something unseen by human eyes had appeared.

Another courthouse worker tells Smith, "I was walking up the steps from the basement one night and I felt something behind me. I looked back and there was no one there. . . . The feeling was too strong to be nothing."

Many workers who believe and have experienced "something" don't want their names known, for fear people would think them "crazy."

Smith and others have speculated as to who the ghost could be. It might be a janitor whose body was found in 1895 at the bottom of the steps leading into the basement. He was in the courthouse performing his nightly duties when he died. Early the next morning another custodian found his lifeless body. The victim's neck was broken. His head showed signs of trauma.

There are just as many questions about his death as there are about the identity of the ghost. Was this an accidental death? Was he pushed to his death? Or, could he have been frightened and lost his footing? It was presumed that his neck was broken and his head battered when he fell down the steps.

Could the janitor be the courthouse ghost? Is it a coincidence that those who've "felt" the presence of the ghost felt it near the basement steps?

Smith offers another theory on the ghost's identity: It might be a man who was strung up to a tree in 1879. He had been acquitted of murder. Later he was arrested on another charge. While he was being held in the county jail, an angry mob stormed the jail, grabbed the man, and then proceeded to lynch him.

She points out a problem to this theory, though: The man was hanged in the jail yard that was more than a block from the courthouse. Thus, she doesn't feel that he could be the ghost.

Why not? He did not get true justice by the law. Where would he then go to seek justice after death? The courthouse, of course. Perhaps he's looking for an attorney to take his case.

GIBSON COUNTY

❖❖❖❖❖❖❖❖❖❖ THE COUNTY was named for Brig. Gen. John Gibson, an Indian fighter and secretary of the Indiana territory (1800–1816). The county has a large coal reserve and a booming oil industry. Oil pumps can be seen in backyards, pastures, cornfields, churchyards, and school grounds.

One of the state's larger coal-fueled, electric-generating stations is located nine miles west of Princeton, the county seat. Princeton was chosen as the county seat because of its central location. Platted in 1814, the town was named for William Prince, the county's first resident attorney, legislature, judge, and congressman.

Economic growth in Princeton had not been steady in the past, but it experienced a surge of industrial development in the 1970s, when Toyota Motor Manufacturing, Inc., located there. As the new century arrived, the truck manufacturing plant had nearly five thousand employees.

Although several commercial buildings surrounding the courthouse square have been renovated, the Greek Candy Store, founded in 1906 at 201 Hart Street, still contains the original soda fountain and mirrored-back bar.

Gibson County is well known for its watermelons and cantaloupes, which are raised in the sandy soils associated with the Owensville and Johnson areas of the county. More than one million dollars worth of melons are raised annually.

Patoka is the county's oldest town, settled in 1789 by John Severns. The town was first called Smithfield, and then renamed Columbia in 1813 at the time it was platted. Shortly thereafter it was renamed for the river. According to local legend, Patoka means "log on the bottom," and applies to the river because there are supposedly several logs stuck in the mud of the river's bottom.

The village of Lyles Station was originally known as Cherry Grove Vicinity. Its name changed after the Civil War, when Joshua Lyles, an African American, purchased several acres of land and began farming. Other blacks came to the area and settled, and eventually the community was renamed for Lyles.

By the turn of the century, Lyles Station was a thriving all-black community with two churches, two general stores, a post office, railroad station, and an elementary school. The devastating 1913 flood was the beginning of the end for the town.

Railroad passenger service ended in 1951, sealing its fate. All that remains are a few farmhouses, a cemetery, a chapel believed to be the only extant rural African Methodist Episcopal Church, and the school building that was built in 1919. In 1999 the Lyles Station School was placed on the list of Historic Places, and in 2001 restoration was begun. ❖

The Ghost of Cockrum Hall

Oakland City is a small farming community of three thousand residents just east of Princeton. In 1866, Oakland Institute was founded, but due to insufficient funds it was forced to close. The state granted a charter in 1885 for the founding of Oakland City College, a private school affiliated with the General Association of General Baptists.

Col. William Monroe Cockrum, a Civil War veteran and prosperous farmer of the community, donated several wooded acres on which the school was built. The first building, constructed of bricks manufactured on the grounds, was completed in 1892.

That building and a later addition form the current Administration Building. The school's name was changed to Oakland City University in 1995.

Sitting on a hill encircled by oak trees is Cockrum Hall, the former residence of Col. and Mrs. William Cockrum. This two-story brick mansion with a large corner tower was built by Col. Cockrum in 1876 in the style of an Italian villa.

The Hall, which was placed on the National Registry of Historic Places in 1978, housed the music department until 1995. Since 1995 the building has remained unoccupied. The *Evansville Courier and Press* announced in a recent article that the building would be restored and utilized for the development and alumni office.

Although the building had been unoccupied by members of the school for some time, it still had a resident—a ghost! Many generations have known and told the tales of a female that haunts Cockrum Hall.

Some accounts surrounding the hauntings tell the tragic tale of a suicide. A distraught woman climbed to the tower and was later found hanging from a rafter. Some believe that the ghost is Lucretia, the wife of Col. Cockrum. Still others believe it is one of Cockrums' daughters.

There is another version that identifies the ghost as a male. If it is a male, who then would it be? According to this version the ghost is Col. Cockrum, who supposedly had been killed by his wife.

In all of these accounts the identity of the ghost is wrong. Col. Cockrum died in 1924, seven years after his wife. Thus, she could not have killed him. Nor did she or any other member of the family commit suicide.

Is Cockrum Hall haunted? Many believe it is. They've had experiences, seen things, and felt something. Those who believe say that sometimes if you look through the windows at night something eerie and unexplainable will be seen. At first it's a faint rosy or pink glow that quickly turns to a bright orange and just as quickly disappears. Before the music school vacated the building, students often reported hearing doors open and close when no one else was in the building.

If none of the Cockrum family is haunting the hall, who is? Could it be a lost soul?

The Princeton Monster

Stories of strange hairy creatures abound throughout the world. Not to be left out, Gibson county has it's own story of encounters with a strange creature.

Near Princeton was an old storage area for oil well drilling, a secluded spot perfect for parking and "contemplation." A familiar location for high school kids to go. Peaceful and private.

All this changed one summer. It became a place of terror. One night a parked couple's car was attacked by something huge. The boy was able to start the engine and, without lights, speed away. Later they described the attacker as being either a big man or a bear.

Several times throughout the summer, others reported encountering this frightful image. Finally a posse was gathered together, determined to discover what was frightening the teenagers.

Armed with rifles, they gathered along the road. Their plan was simple. They'd park their cars so they could turn headlights on whenever the creature appeared, blinding it as you would a deer. And, if need be, they'd shoot to kill!

They didn't have long to wait long until a shadow was seen coming from the woods. Anxious to see what was approaching, headlights began illuminating the darkness.

Whatever it was, it was reported to be seven or eight feet tall, standing upright, and covered with long hair. Startled by the bright headlights, it began to run, heading for the protection of the woods.

Shots rang out time and time again. And then, silence. Shaken and confused, the posse returned to Princeton to report their encounter with the monster. They all agreed that it could not have been a bear. It couldn't have been a man, could it? If not, then what? An unknown creature—a monster!

The next morning with the sun brightly shining, the men along with many curious townspeople returned to the spot of their en-counter. There, on the roadway and leading into the woods, they found blood. A few men dared to follow the traces of blood into the woods until they lost the trail—or until they became too fearful to continue.

No trace of the monster was found—dead or alive. Was it an animal of some kind? A wild man from prehistoric times? A Hoosier Yeti or Sasquatch? Imagination? If imagination, how could the blood be explained? All who experienced encounters with the Princeton monster swear it did happen, but after that night the monster never again terrorized those who dared to park at the location of the old storage area.

The Gibson County encounters, however, are not the only reports in Indiana of such creatures called "Bigfoot." Sightings of the creature have been reported in numerous counties through-out the state. The description is universally the same, with only minor differences. Could there be such a creature as Bigfoot here in Indiana?

Until there is proof that it exists, Bigfoot remains a part of Indiana's folklore.

JEFFERSON COUNTY

❖❖❖❖❖❖❖❖❖❖ THE COUNTY, organized in 1811, was named for Thomas Jefferson. It's not blessed with fertile soil, abundant minerals, surface water, or lakes. What it does have is a picturesque landscape and significant historic communities that attract sightseers. Nonresidents probably know Jefferson County for its annual powerboat regatta, Clifty Falls State Park, and historical architecture.

Madison, named for President James Madison, was laid out in 1810. Built on river bottomland at the uppermost part of a horseshoe bend in the Ohio River, Madison is ringed by rock cliffs and hills that rise up to four hundred feet above the community.

From 1830 to 1855, Madison experienced its golden era as influence and affluence came its way. A major key was the completion of transportation projects that tied the city to the rest of the region. The connecting of river, road, and railroad into a comprehensive system placed Madison at the funnel end of a continuous flow of raw materials. The town assumed a major role in Indiana's antebellum economic welfare by being the terminus of the Michigan Road, which extended from Michigan City to Madison, as well as by being the headquarters of Indiana's first commercial railroad, the Madison and Indianapolis.

The building of the Madison and Indianapolis railroad was an engineering feat of some magnitude. The route ascended the high north ridge behind Madison. The roadbed was cut deep into the limestone hills producing an incline more than 1.3 miles in length and rising three feet per mile. It was one of the steepest standard-gauge railroads ever built in the United States.

At first, horses and oxen were used to pull the cars one by one to the top of the incline, where the train was then reassembled. From 1844 to 1868 locomotives were used with a rack-and-pinion system. From 1868 to 1905 a fifty-five-ton engine towed the cars up the grade without the use of cogwheels.

Madison's cultural star ascended in the early twentieth century, when renowned Hoosier author and historian Edward Eggleston became a resident and active participant in library affairs.

Residents of Madison and Jefferson Counties subscribed enough money in 1920 to purchase and present to the state Clifty Falls and several surrounding acres for the establishment of a state park. Several waterfalls lie within the rugged natural beauty of this area.

The state's first historical memorial, Madison's Lanier mansion, opened to the public in 1926. The Greek Classic-style house was built in 1844 for J.F.D. Lanier, first president of the Indiana State Bank of Madison. In 1925, the home was bought and restored as a tribute to Mr. Lanier in recognition of his services to Indiana during the Civil War.

In 1940 the government began building the Jefferson Proving Grounds north of Madison. When completed, the project took in 56,000 acres and spread into parts of three counties. About five hundred families were uprooted, twenty-one cemeteries were reburied, five towns were ab-sorbed, and four schools and two churches were closed. It took only forty-five days to depopulate the area. In 1989 the Proving Ground was closed.

The Annual Madison Regatta, begun in 1949, is one of the most well known powerboat events on the Ohio River. It achieved national status in 1952 when it was sanctioned by the American Power Boat Association.

Madison continued to be a national focus when Hollywood came to town. It was the setting for the award-winning 1959 release of *Some Came Running*, starring Frank Sinatra, Dean Martin, Shirley MacLaine, Arthur Kennedy, and Martha Hyer.

Madison's warranted reputation as one of Indiana's most beautiful and most cared-for cities seems secure. Even now, the city's seasoned menu of attractions, including the annual Chautauqua of the Arts, the Regatta, the Tour of Homes, and the Christmas Candlelight Tour, continues to draw huge crowds to the "Williamsburg of the West." ❖

Haunted Hanover

Hanover College is located on the Ohio River, six miles from Madison. Established in 1827, it is the oldest private college in Indiana. The beautiful 650-acre campus with its thirty-four Georgian-styled buildings sits on a high plateau, five hundred feet above the Ohio River, providing an extensive and glorious panoramic view of the river and its rich valley.

Hanover's Parker Auditorium was built in 1947 and named for former college president Albert Parker, Jr. Today the building is the home of the college's theater department and the site of many productions. The auditorium seats 750 people. Students and em-ployees say, however, that there would actually be 751 patrons in attendance.

Parker became Hanover's president in 1929. The school, like so many other institutions, was suffering from financial problems due to the Great Depression. Enrollment had dropped, and the school was feeling the financial pinch. One of the first things Parker did was to start a fund-raising campaign to help turn things around.

Two years after Parker's death in 1958, stories of hauntings in the auditorium began circulating.

A theater graduate shared with his friends his belief that he'd actually seen Parker's ghost. One night, while performing, he had a few minutes offstage and decided to get a drink of water.

While on his way to the water fountain, he encountered a middle-aged man standing in the shadows at the back of the auditorium, watching. It struck him as strange. As he retraced his steps he discovered the man was gone. At that time he didn't give too much thought to the matter.

On another occasion the same student had a work session scheduled at the theater on a Saturday morning. He was the first to arrive and had to use his keys to enter. As he was in the scenery shop below the stage, he heard a loud scraping coming from above. Going up the stairs to see who was there, he found no one. Both the stage and the auditorium were completely deserted.

The student didn't initially share his experiences and suspicions until others began telling of strange happenings in Parker Auditorium—a man's voice being heard and yet no one was there, loud sounds coming from the stage area, missing items, and sightings of what appeared to be a middle-aged man standing in the shadows who would disappear when approached. Could it be President Parker?

JENNINGS COUNTY

❖❖❖❖❖❖❖❖❖❖THE STATE'S seventeenth county was named for Jonathan Jennings, Indiana's first governor (1816–1822). Vernon, founded in 1815 by John Vawter (1782–1862), a Baptist minister, was chosen two years later to be the Jennings County seat. It is believed that the town is named for George Washington's home, Mt. Vernon. The town is located on a plateau almost surrounded by a loop of the Muscatatuck River, which essentially precluded any outward growth.

Of political interest, Vernon's 1851 Act of Incorporation granted it jurisdiction over its election laws. Elections are held every two years in March, bucking the statewide practice of November elections every four years.

The town has several buildings dating back to its earliest beginnings. Located on the corner of Pile and Brown Streets, just north of the courthouse, is possibly the oldest building, the North American House. Erected in 1820, just three years after Vernon became the county seat, the building operated as an inn and stagecoach stop. Today it is the home of Our Heritage, Inc., Jennings County's Historical Society.

Among the pioneer gravesites in the Vernon Cemetery can be found those of Wilbur Shaw, three-time winner of the Indianapolis 500 (1937, 1934, 1940) who died in a plane crash in 1954 at the age of fifty-two, and Pat O'Connor, another Indianapolis 500 driver who was killed in a fourteen-car pileup on the first lap of the 1958 race.

The Crosley State Fish and Wildlife Area was given to the state in 1958. The property contains a diverse topography of upland forest, lakes, ponds, caves, and cliffs. Within its boundaries is the Baldwin Cemetery. A path from the cemetery through the woods leads to the re-mains of Tunnel Mill, perhaps Jennings County's most significant historical asset.

In 1824 Ebenezer Baldwin created the mill, which features a two-hundred-foot tunnel that was dug from the solid bedrock of the ridge that divides the Muscatatuck River, whose waters create a near oxbow in the geography. A dam was built to channel the river through the tunnel to power the mill's turbine. The Tunnel Mill was considered to be "an extraordinary engineering feat for its time," and according to the Indiana Department of Natural Re-sources survey of historical structures, the site is "one of the most remarkable industrial structures of pioneer days." Today all that remains of the original mill is a corner of the southwest walls, the chimney, and the tunnel.

Butlerville, platted in 1853, derived its name from its first postmaster's hometown of Butlerville, Ohio. Two notable personalities have close ties with the town. Jessamyn West (1902–1984)—author of more than a dozen novels, including *Friendly Persuasion* (1945), the story of an Indiana Quaker family in 1862, which became a movie in 1956 starring Gary Cooper and Dorothy McGuire—was born in Butlerville and lived there until age six, when her family moved to California. She was a cousin to former President Richard Milhouse Nixon, whose roots go deep in Jennings County.

The great-grandparents of Nixon and West, Elizabeth and Joshua Milhouse, moved to the county from Ohio in 1854. The devout Quakers (Elizabeth was a Quaker minister) settled on a farm south of Butlerville on Rush Branch Creek. Nixon's mother, Hannah, was born in 1885 to Franklin and Almira Milhouse on a farm adjacent to the West farm. Nixon is one of two presidents, Benjamin Harrison being the other, to have had a Hoosier-born parent. ❖

Little Boy Lost

The Jennings County Historical Society is located in the North American House, at 134 East Brown Street in Vernon. Thomas J. Storey built the house in 1838. During its lifetime it has served as a stagecoach stop, residence, inn, and the Storey Pharmacy.

Today at the Jennings County Historical Society museum, it's possible to take a trip back in time and enjoy a visit with a little boy from the past. His name is Matthew Philips.

Before Thomas Storey came to town and decided to build his house, there was nothing on the site but a field. This was a perfect place for children to play when their chores were done. One late afternoon a group of young boys were playing in the field, and among them was eight-year-old Matthew Philips. As Matthew was running across the field, his friends in hot pursuit, he suddenly disappeared before their eyes, as if the earth had swallowed him up. And, indeed it had!

Young Matthew had fallen into a deep hole that had been hidden in the grass. A spring-fed sinkhole. It wasn't a wide hole, but it was just wide enough for a young boy to slip into.

His friends heard him screaming for help as he struggled to free himself to no avail, sinking deeper and deeper into the earth. As fast as they could his friends sounded the alarm.

His parents and neighbors came running. The only chance they had to save him was for someone to be lowered into the sinkhole by rope. The task was too dangerous for a child, and the hole was too small for an adult. Frantically, they began digging to widen the opening.

The sun set and darkness set in. Lanterns and torches were lit as the community continued frantically digging. Finally, early the next morning his father was lowered on a rope into the hole. Often when people fall into spring-fed sink holes, they can be carried underground through a system of streams and never found. This was not the case with young Matthew. Reaching into the ice-cold spring water, the father found his son. The grief-stricken father, with his arms tightly wrapped around his son's lifeless body, was brought to the surface.

The townspeople covered the hole to ensure that this tragedy would never happen again. Some years passed, and then Storey came to Vernon and, on the ground where young Matthew and his friends had played, he built a stagecoach stop he named the North American House. The sinkhole where Matthew had died became a well. For several years the Storey family owned and lived in the house.

As time passed the house became vacant and fell into disuse. The museum took over the site, renovating the building and opening it to the public. That's when the stories began.

Volunteers reported hearing the sound of feet, like those of a small child, walking through the museum when no child was there. Other strange and unexplained things began to happen. When the museum was unlocked each morning, workers began noticing the beds in some of the exhibits were rumpled, as if they'd been slept in.

Those connected with the museum soon accepted the fact that the North American House was the home of young Matthew Philips's spirit. Some visitors to the museum have been a little frightened when they've encountered Matthew, hearing his footsteps following them through the exhibits. Some of these visitors have even heard childish laughter.

Contrary Mary

Just outside of Vernon lays the Crosley State Fish and Wildlife Area. In 1958, the Indiana Department of Natural Resources (*idnr*) purchased the large tract of land, 4,084 acres, with an upland forest, lakes, ponds, caves, and cliffs. Within this vast area is the Tunnel Mill, on a ridge near the Muscatatuck River oxbow.

Ebenezer Baldwin created this mill in 1824. It features a two-hundred-foot tunnel dug from solid bedrock. He then constructed a dam to channel the river through the tunnel to power the mill.

The remnants of the original mill lie on the most northern fringe along a ridge near the Muscatatuck River. The tunnel and a corner of the southwest wall and chimney are all that's left.

The Baldwin pioneer cemetery can also be found within the IDNR property. The cemetery served the area for a very long time and is the final resting place of several early settlers, including Mary Smith.

Mary and her sister, Gladys, grew up in Vernon. Gladys was outgoing, talkative, and fun-loving, while Mary was extremely shy, quiet, and withdrawn. Because of the extreme differences between the two girls, Mary became the subject of gossip. As she grew older, the rumors became more inventive and vicious. Mary became even more isolated as a means to protect herself from the cruel world. This only made people talk more and become increasingly creative in their stories.

Many of the residents in Vernon were convinced that Mary was a witch. She silently endured their taunts and humiliations. Through it all, Gladys defended her sister as best she could. After their parents died, the two girls found themselves living alone in the family home.

One night in 1837, as the legend states, Mary was home alone. She'd already changed into her white nightgown and was ready to retire when she realized she needed more wood for the fire.

She opened the door and walked outside toward the woodpile. As she approached, Mary was pushed to the ground. Rolling over, she tried to defend herself. The assailant, viscously wielding his knife, quickly put an end to poor Mary's life. She was laid to rest in the peaceful Baldwin Cemetery.

This is not the end of the story, however. About five years after her death, a drunk who was stumbling around the burial ground tripped and fell on her grave. The drunk could only gasp and stare when Mary's spirit rose from the grave, a specter in a flowing white gown. Running from the cemetery, the man returned to the town and told of his fearful encounter.

The contrary Mary will not stay in her grave. More than a century has passed since her death. There are those who swear her ghost can still be seen sitting on a stump near her gravesite. Anyone who dares to approach will not get close; they feel the violence of her murder hanging in the air and can go no farther. In fact, they run for their lives.

Contrary Mary's gravesite. PHOTO: Jonathan Tétreault

MONROE COUNTY

❖·❖·❖·❖·❖·❖·❖·❖·❖ THE LAND THAT WOULD
become Monroe County was put on sale in September
1816, and it soon became very popular territory. The
county was formed in 1818 and named for the fifth president of the United States, James Monroe.

President James Madison had wanted to create a
township in the new state that would be known as a
"Seminary of Learning." That designation was assigned
to Township Eight North, Range One West—now known
as Perry Township—and that Seminary of Learning
has grown to become Indiana University, the largest in
the nation.

A five-member commission was appointed to locate
a site for the county seat. After locating what they con-si-
dered to be the best spot, in 1815 the commission
purchased 160 acres from David Rogers for one hundred
dollars and an additional 150 acres from Robertson
Graham for nine hundred dollars. The area was platted
in 1818 and named Bloomington. According to legend,
the name was suggested when a group of early settlers
were impressed by the numerous wildflowers carpeting
the area. ❖

The Ghosts of Indiana University

Indiana University was founded in 1820 at Bloomington and
is one of the oldest institutions of higher education west of the
Allegheny Mountains. With nearly 100,000 full- and part-time
students on eight campuses, as well as a faculty of more than four
thousand, it is one of the largest universities in the nation. So it's

not surprising that there'd be a few school spirits floating around the legendary campus—school spirits of the ghostly type.

One of the several haunting legends is placed at McNutt Quad. Several years ago two female students did not go home for the winter holiday, but stayed at the dorm.

Late one night one of the girls decided to go downstairs to get some food. While she was gone, a news flash came on the radio warning everyone that there was an escaped lunatic on the loose in the area armed with a hatchet.

The roommate got up and checked to make sure the door was locked and then began to wait for her friend to return. Fifteen minutes went by. A half hour. Finally, an hour had passed and the girl had not returned.

Then the roommate heard a strange sound coming from the hallway. A dragging, thumping sound, and then a faint scratching that seemed to be coming from just outside the dorm room door. Terrified, she huddled in the room. The sounds in the hall ceased, and all was quiet.

As the night wore on she continued to wait for her friend's re-turn. Exhausted and unable to keep her eyes open, she fell asleep.

The next morning she was awoken by the sound of pounding on her door and a voice saying that it was the police. Cautiously, she opened the door. There in the hallway, in a pool of blood, lay her roommate. She had been killed by blows from a hatchet.

As the story goes, the murderer was never caught.

Another legendary tale involves of the most haunted sites on campus, Read Hall. Its stories date back to when the building was an all-female dorm.

It was formal night. The girl was wearing a yellow gown. It was very late when she and her boyfriend arrived back at her dorm, Read Hall. Although it had been an idyllic night, the girl in the yellow dress had chosen this night to tell her boyfriend, a medical student, she wanted to break up with him.

He had been unaware of her decision. Thinking that the night had been perfect, he was taken by surprise when she told him she no longer wanted to be a part of his life. She ended his pleadings to reconsider when she entered the dormitory and shut the door, leaving him standing alone in the darkness.

She had reached her room when suddenly her boyfriend leaped at her. How he entered the dorm and her room is not known. But there he was in a murderous rage. Before she could let out a scream, he had slit her throat!

He carried her body down to the boiler room, where he hid her along with the murder weapon—a scalpel.

Sightings have been reported for many years of a girl wearing a yellow dress or nightgown walking the halls of Read.

A residential assistant at Read recalled her encounter with the girl in yellow during the summer of 2002. Before the semester started, she and another R.A. were hanging bulletin boards in the part of the dorms where all the halls intersect. They had propped open all the doors, but they kept slamming shut. Each time, the girls would turn around, and out of the corner of their eyes they'd see a yellow nightgown. They were so scared they couldn't finish their project and had to leave the area.

Residents of Read have also had similar encounters. A freshman told of the strange happenings in her room at Read. She would be alone in the room, when suddenly the bathroom door would slam shut. It could not have been the wind, because either the window wasn't open or, if it were, there was no breeze coming through. Sometimes this phenomenon would happen when her roommate was in the room, but asleep.

Unlike when the murder occurred, Read is now coed—and the paranormal activity is not confined to just the girls' rooms. One male student living in the dorm had several strange experiences that usually took place early in the morning. The door to his room would be locked, and yet, around two in the morning it would open wide and slam against the wall. He'd jump out of bed and look out into the hallway, and no one would be there. This happened more than once. He also swears that during the summer his room would have unexplained drastic temperature changes. First it would be really warm, then it would suddenly get really cold for no reason, and then it would get warm again.

Also located on the IU campus, one of Bloomington's most famous haunted spots is the Career Development Center (CDC). The legend behind this haunting can't be traced to a specific date, but it is believed it started sometime before World War *ii*.

The CDC building was built sometime during the first half of the twentieth century. The original owner, it's said, shot himself in the basement. This then might have begun the long haunted history of the house. The next owner was a doctor, known for performing behind-closed-door abortions for a number of coeds.

According to legend, the doctor would hide aborted fetuses in the basement wall behind a steel door, or he'd burn them in an oven in the basement, where the abortions were often performed.

This continued until one day something terrible happened during an abortion procedure. The young patient died. While it had been easy to hide an unknown, unborn baby, it was a different matter altogether to hide the death of a young woman who had a name, an identity, family, and friends.

The doctor was arrested. Posting bail, he returned to his home, and there, from the top banister of the spiral staircase, he hung himself.

In 1944, IU purchased the house. Since that time it's been home to sororities, fraternities, the Environmental, Health, and Safety Management offices, and others, until its current occupation by the CDC.

Since the house became a part of the vast IU campus, strange sightings have occured and tales have been told by the various inhabitants.

A fraternity member believes he actually came in contact with the doctor. It was the weekend, and he was alone in the house when he heard footsteps on the floor above him. He called out, but no one answered. He climbed up the spiral staircase to the second floor to search for the source of the sound. Finding no one, he returned to the stairs. Just as he reached them, he felt a tap on his shoulder. He quickly turned around—again no one was there.

Other strange events have been reported in the building, such as faucets turning on and off without the aid of a human hand. One student even reported that he walked into his bathroom late one night to find a man washing his hands. The man turned, walked past the student, and left. In a state of disbelief, the student followed him out into the hallway, and as the man neared the spiral stairs, he vanished into thin air.

Perhaps the most chilling stories often told about the house, however, concern the many aborted babies the doctor supposedly hid in the walls. Through the years there have been numerous reports from people who have heard the ghostly sounds of babies whimpering and crying. Those intrepid investigators who dared to seek out the source of the sounds agree they grew louder as they entered the basement.

Another haunted site at the school is the Indiana Memorial Union (IMU), which was dedicated at the June 13, 1932 Commencement, to "the sons and daughters of Indiana University who had served in the wars of the Republic." With 500,000 square feet of space, the IMU is one of the largest student unions in the world.

The venerable, elegant Tudor-style building has a few ethereal surprises tucked among its antiques and priceless art works. In the second floor Federal Room, with its hand-produced wallpaper representing tourist impressions of early nineteenth century America, you will find the unfinished portrait of Mary Burney.

Burney, an art critic, didn't approve of how the portrait was being painted. Before changes could be made, she died in a fire with her husband and son.

Legend holds that building managers have noticed some of the valuables missing from the enclosed cabinets in the room. Originally placed near the painting were two urns containing the ashes of Burney's husband and son. Both of these have mysteriously disappeared. On occasion, especially if someone was alone, the smell of Burney's perfume filled the room.

Students and visitors alike agree that it's easy to feel comfortable in this room when you're not alone. But if you do find yourself alone in the room, you can feel Burney's presence and get a whiff of her perfume. Is it possible that Burney is still watching and waiting for her portrait to be finished?

The building's Tudor Room is famous for its weekend brunch, and through the week, guests and students alike can enjoy a luxurious lunch buffet. But there's more to the elegant dining room than can be seen.

Several student staff members are aware of a mischievous spirit they call Jacob. On any given day when the staff returns to work, they may find the white table linens flung about and the table services all mixed up, after the table setting had been neatly arranged for the next day's luncheon.

Among the many canvases that adorn the venerable and very staid dining area is one by O.O. Haig, titled *Halloween*. It depicts a sweet-faced child holding a jack-o'-lantern. The students believe this is the portrait of Jacob. His picture may depict him as an an-gelic child, but evidently he is not all that angelic.

It is this child whom Tudor Room staff believe comes alive after hours. Besides the disrupted table settings, he is often blamed for vases of flowers being overturned and other devilish tricks. When the fifteenth century tapestries were removed to be cleaned, Jacob put up quite a fuss that is still remembered. But no one will talk about it to outsiders.

Although not too many students report supernatural encounters at the IMU, custodians swear that the older portion of the building is haunted. Late at night, maintenance people will turn off the lights in the Bryan Room, only to find that someone, or something, has mysteriously turned the lights back on. This will happen as many as five times in a single night.

The custodians report that most of the paranormal activity is centered around the west wing's fifth floor, where the elevator has been known to mysteriously stop. One custodian was on the fifth floor one night just after midnight when he heard talking coming over his security radio. He called everyone to see if anyone was calling him, but no one was. As he turned toward the elevator, he felt a cold breeze and saw the dark shadow of a man running past him. Needless to say, the custodian was truly spooked.

In 1973 Indiana University acquired a building to house the Latino Cultural Center, La Casa. Little is known about the building. But one thing is certain: It, too, is haunted, but by a ghost not intent on frightening people.

La Casa Director Lillian Casillas says that several student staff members have seen the shadowy silhouette of what they believed to be a woman, walking around on the second floor. Casillas herself admits that she's heard the sounds of a typewriter when there was no one around.

Some time in October 2002, Casillas says a student was about to lock up when the sounds of someone running upstairs were heard. Upon checking, the student found that no one was there.

Nobody at the center has any idea as to the identity of the mysterious female ghost or why she haunts the building.

Could she be related to the mysterious woman in black who has been seen on campus since 1911? At that time, she was often reported roaming Third Street. According to reports from the IU archives, the specter eventually made an appearance at a Women's League Halloween party and announced that she would return to haunt Third Street every Halloween night.

She is described as a large woman in black with a very big black umbrella. Some say that she has been known to chase students, brandishing her umbrella in a menacing manner.

Another figure of note, Chancellor Herman B. Wells was a legend in his own time and seems destined to always be part of Indiana University's legends. After sixty-three years of dedicating his love and life to the school, he passed away on March 18, 2000, at the august age of ninety-eight.

Prior to his death, plans were already underway to create a statute in his likeness to be placed in the center of the campus. At the dedication ceremonies in October 2000, IU President Myles Brand said, "While death ends a life, it does not end a relationship. Herman Wells' relationship with IU will remain vital for generations to come."

The sculpture was created by Professor Langland of the IU South Bend fine arts department, who chose to represent Wells in his prime—in his late sixties or early seventies—sitting on an IU park bench, apparently resting after a casual walk through his beloved campus. Wells's right hand is extended, ready to shake hands with anyone who comes by. He's relaxed and content. The statue is very lifelike, perhaps too lifelike. The statue wasn't in place a month be-fore the legends about it began to surface. There have been reports of people seeing Wells move his hand, as if in greeting.

Herman Wells statue on the campus of Indiana University. PHOTO: Jason Lourie

POSEY COUNTY

❖❖❖❖❖❖❖❖❖❖ THE COUNTY, organized in 1814, was named in honor of Revolutionary soldier Maj. Gen. Thomas Posey (1750–1818). Because of its commercially advantageous position on the Ohio River, Mount Vernon was selected as the county seat. The town, originally known as McFadden's Bluff or McFadden's Landing, was settled by Andrew McFadden in about 1805, and was first platted by John Waggoner in 1818. The name was changed to honor the home of Gen. George Washington.

But for a time, Mount Vernon was also known as Hoop-Pole Township. River traffic was brisk, as flatboats, piled high with produce and grain, plied the waters of the Ohio River on their way to the New Orleans markets. A stopover at "Slim" Andy's wharf at Mount Vernon brought welcome rest and a chance for refreshments at one of the two taverns.

The professional river boatmen were a colorful, hard-drinking, rough and tumble sort. Strong and courageous, they loved to fight and would often do so just for fun. About 1832, so the story goes, a half-dozen flatboats were tied up at the wharf while the rivermen enjoyed themselves at John Carson's saloon.

Workers from an adjacent cooper shop strolled in for a bit of refreshment. Apparently for no reason at all, the rivermen picked a fight with the local men, who were badly beaten. When some of the other men in town heard of the ruckus and defeat of their neighbors and friends, they armed themselves with hoop-poles (wooden staffs made of saplings used in making barrels) from the near-by cooper shop and converged on the rivermen. The fight was waged with such intensity that the bruised and bloody boatmen were glad to flee back to their boats. All the way up and down the Ohio, the news traveled of the hoop-pole fight. For many years after, Mount Vernon was considered a rough and tough river town and referred to as "Hoop-Pole Township."

One of the most unique areas in the state is the Hovey Lake State Fish and Wildlife Area. The area was first designated in 1940 with the purchase of 885 acres, but was later increased to 4,298 acres, many of which are under water. The preserve is noted for its stand of bald cypress trees, believed to be one of the northernmost stands in the United States. The tall hardwoods are usually found in the bottomlands of the South. The trees rising from the water and shoreline of Hovey Lake create the appearance of a primeval swamp.

Since the construction of the Uniontown Locks and Dam, Hovey Lake's water level has significantly raised. Many of the cypress trees have died because their "knees" were submerged year-round. The Department of Natural Resources began planting hundreds of young cypress on higher ground surrounding the lake in an effort to save this natural legacy. Other plants found in the area are pecan trees, southern red oak, swamp privet, and mistletoe.

New Harmony, settled in 1814, was the site of two radical experiments in communal living during the first half of the nineteenth century. The first of these began with a small group of Lutheran dissenters led by George Rap (1757–1847), who came up the White River by flat boat and founded the community as Harmonie. The group had left Germany in 1805 and had settled in Butler County, Pennsylvania, until they purchased the land in Posey County.

The society labored to create a cooperative community bound by the principles of celibacy, obedience, and Christian communal living. Convinced they were the chosen people, they prepared for the Second Coming of Christ in their lifetime. The Harmonists cultivated 1,450 acres of land and built a community of 180 log-and-brick buildings, some of which still stand.

In 1824, Rapp advertised to sell the society's 20,000 acres with an asking price of, $150,000. Robert Dale Owen purchased the holding in 1825, and Rapp led his followers back to Pennsylvania.

Rapp's Harmonie became the site of Owen's utopian experiment, which was renamed New Harmony. In 1825 Robert Dale Owen (1771–1857), a Welsh industrialist, socialist, and philanthropist, along with William McClure (1763– 1840), a Scottish philanthropist, founded this new social order. They assembled a group of renowned teachers and scientists from all disciplines who came to the area aboard what was referred to as the "Boatload of Knowledge."

Owen dissolved his community in 1827 and returned to Scotland. His children and many participants remained. New Harmony basked in a cultural and scientific exhilaration until the 1850s.

The Owenites, believing that education was the key to a new and better life, made many contributions to society, among them: America's first kindergarten, first infant school, first trade school, first public school system offering equal education for both sexes, first free library, first civic dramatic club, and the first headquarters of the U.S. Geological Society.

Historic New Harmony Inc., a nonprofit preservation group managed by the University of Southern Indiana at Evansville, conducts walking tours of the nearly two-dozen historic buildings from both of these experiments.

William McClure also was interested in the education of the working class and, at his death, provided a certain portion of his estate to be used for the establishment of "Working Men's Libraries." Robb Township, in which Poseyville is located, received the sum of five hundred dollars. A two-room cottage was rented, and a selection of books, purchased. In 1905 Andrew Carnegie provided the funds to build the Poseyville library, which still is being used today. ❖

The Weeping Woman of Old Hoop-Pole Township

Soon it will be two centuries since the discovery and settling of McFadden's Bluff, today's Mount Vernon. For a time the community was known as "Hoop-Pole Township." This name was bestowed on the town when some riverboat men tied up at "Slim" Andy's wharf for rest and refreshments at one of the local taverns. The boatmen were well known to be boisterous bullies who loved to fight for the sake of fighting. They picked a fight with some local coopers, who got the worst of it. When other townsmen heard of the thrashing of their friends and neighbors, they went to the coopers' shop, armed themselves with hoop-poles (saplings used in making barrels), and challenged the burly rivermen. This time the victory went to the Mt. Vernon men. The bruised and bloodied rivermen were glad to leave with their lives. The story of the hoop-pole fight became well known. Mount Vernon acquired the reputation of being a rough and tumble town known as "Hoop-Pole Township."

In October 1993 an article appeared in the *Mt. Vernon Democrat* recounting the tale of the Weeping Woman of Old Hoop-Pole Township. Before sharing with readers this haunting tale, however, the author recalled the panic and fear among the residents of the town's West End some time during 1907 when another mysterious entity, "Black Annie," a witch, roamed the streets after nightfall. In fear, young and old stayed in their homes behind tightly-locked doors. Finally a few brave men armed with guns confronted the black-clad witch. Once threatened, the witch pulled off her long black shawl to disclose that the "she" was a "he" with only a prankish nature.

Not so harmless, though, was the Weeping Woman of Old Hoop-Pole Township, who frightened and kept the settlers awake night after night in the early years of the settlement. She was seen by few, but heard by nearly all.

The unnamed woman's story was one of insanity and tragedy. The general belief among the pioneers was that in a fit of insanity on a dark and stormy night, she'd tossed her two children into the raging waters of the Ohio River. In that insane state, she wasn't aware of what she'd done, but knowing her children were gone, she roamed the countryside weeping and wailing, and calling over and over again, "Where are my children? Oh where, where are my children?"

Throughout the year, summer or winter, from nightfall until dawn, her pitiful, piercing shrieks were heard almost nightly by many of the settlers.

Then came the night of December 16, 1811, the night of the earthquake in New Madrid, Missouri. The tremors shook the Midwest, changing the course of the rivers and creating lakes where none had been.

It was a cold night. A thin blanket of snow covered the ground. A full winter's moon illuminated the night. All was quiet in the little village by the river until midnight, when the familiar shrieks, "Where are my children? Oh, where, where are my children?" were heard. The sound came from what was known as Mulberry Hill and continued for almost an hour—and then came the earthquake.

Mulberry Hill shuddered from top to bottom. The Ohio River lashed in a raging fury, and the earth heaved under the feet of the frightened settlers, who ran out of their cabins in sheer panic. The night was filled with screams, crying, shouting, cattle bawling, horses whining, and dogs howling in untold fright.

In one early settler's account, he wrote that ". . . tables and chairs turned over and all of us knocked out of bed. The roar I thought would leave us deaf, if we lived. All you could hear was screams from people and animals. It was the worst thing that I have ever witnessed. It was still dark and you could not see nothing. You could not hold onto nothing neither."

Cabins were set ablaze by toppled lanterns and the sparks of fireplaces. The Weeping Woman was forgotten in the confusion, though she was seen standing silently atop the hill, outlined against the eerie sky, gazing down upon the bedlam below. Just then another cabin burst into flames, the smoke, blaze, and sparks shooting skyward.

Drawing her cape closely about her and covering her head, she ran down the hill. Fighting to stay on their feet and struggling to help their loved, ones no one attempted to stop her as she swiftly entered and darted through the village until she reached the burning cabin. There, she grabbed two small children in her arms and dashed out into the night of chaos and up the hill. She and the children, for one brief moment, were seen silhouetted against the winter sky—and then they disappeared.

After that horrible fateful night in 1811, the Weeping Woman of Hoop-Pole Township was never heard or seen again. The fate of the two children she'd saved is not known.

Poseyville's Haunted Library

Until recently, the Poseyville Carnegie Public Library's claim to fame has been that it's believed to belong to the smallest community ever to receive one of Andrew Carnegie's libraries.

For many years, the library had remained the same as it was when it was built in 1905. Eventually it outgrew the original building. To the south of the library stood the historic Hansbrough Inn, built in 1890, which was being used by the library for storage. In 2000 it was decided to demolish the inn in order to give the library room for expansion.

The library with its new addition was rededicated in October 2000. That's when strange things began happening. Patrons, staff, and volunteers began reporting feeling as if someone were watching them, as if they were not alone, and yet when they looked around, they wouldn't see anyone near them.

Haunted libraries are not unique. Several states report mysteries and strange happenings going on in their stacks. Poseyville's library is only one of the libraries in Indiana to experience this strange phenomenon. Another, one which is not familiar to most people, is the old Tell City Library. Probably, however, Indiana's most famous haunted library is Evansville's Willard Library (see page 208). Several of the nation's haunted libraries, including Willard, have set up "ghost cams" to monitor the library around the clock. Some of these cameras can be viewed on the Internet.

Those at the Poseyville library who have experienced paranormal occurrences believe that the haunting is being done by one of the earliest librarians who, although deceased, still feels a sense of responsibility.

Library Assistant Sheryl Taylor was the first to report something strange going on at the library. Along with her normal librarian duties, she is also responsible for cleaning the library after everyone has gone home. This often requires her to be alone in the locked building late in the evenings.

One evening, she was deep in her thoughts as she went about her cleaning duties when she heard the sound of someone entering the building. There were only three keys to the building: hers, the computer technician's, and the director's. So, she assumed it was either the computer technician or the director, but neither announced his arrival to the building. She went to investigate and found the door was locked and she was alone. Since that first night, the same thing has happened many times during the past three years.

Where the librarian's desk is located, it's impossible to see who comes into the building before you hear them. Thus, a security camera has been placed to show the main entrance and hallway. Even with this camera none, of the librarians have caught a glimpse of the ghost entering or leaving the building.

All the employees have more or less accepted the ghostly visits as a part of their daily routine. Director Stanley Melburn Campbell even admits to bidding the ghost goodnight as he leaves the building.

Taylor is one of the employees who believes this female ghost was originally associated with the library. "I never have the feeling that she, herself, wants to leave or that she wants me to leave. She just wants me to know that she is present." The ghost just may be a librarian from the past—but there also may be more than one ghost.

It was the winter of 2001 when the female ghost first allowed herself to be seen. Taylor was alone in the library. She needed to take some boxes to the area of the basement that was part of the original library. She always felt uncomfortable when she had to go there and it was no different this evening. She didn't want to go down there, but she knew it was something she had to do.

Either from apprehension or imagination, she felt something un-settling in the air. She placed the boxes on the floor and turned to go upstairs. As she turned she thought she saw something. She hurried to the stairs when all of a sudden she thought she could see someone, like a blur, behind her on the stairs. "I looked over my shoulder again and that's when I saw her, a matronly woman surrounded by a hazy mist," recalled Taylor. "She was dressed from an older era."

Since the initial encounter with the ghost, Taylor acknowledges that when she's alone in the library going about her duties, she is aware that the lady is following her about. As she leaves for the night, she senses that the lady walks with her to the door as if to say, "Goodnight and come back."

Taylor's encounter would not be the only one. One evening just before closing, Stanley Forzley, the library's computer technician, had taken a box of computer parts to the basement when he noticed what he described as a column of gray smoke in the far northeastern corner. At first he thought the sump pump had caught fire. Then he realized that, unlike smoke from a fire that would go upward or spread, what he was watching seemed to hover in one spot. Then it vanished. He now feels certain that he, too, saw the library's ghost.

How long the ghost has haunted the lower level of the library is a mystery. Prior to 1998, the library was rarely occupied during evening hours and people ventured into the basement area.

As the renovation and construction got underway, one of the contractors moved an old desk and discovered an early black-and-white photograph of the library. This was a significant find. Most of all the original furniture as it appeared in the photograph still remained in the library. Using this photograph, it was possible to reconstruct one room exactly as it had been in the library's earliest years.

Perhaps this is why the resident ghost feels comfortable in letting the librarians know of her existence. The surroundings are much as they were when she worked in the library.

But in other ways, the library has very much moved into the twenty-first century. There are twelve computers scattered throughout the building. Four of these are located in the old Carnegie section and constantly have problems. Forzley can't explain the source of the mysterious glitches, saying, "I can be putting in a program one minute and suddenly it's gone. Network connections working completely fine one day have to be reestablished the next."

In addition to the computer problems, any diskettes left unattended in that area appear to develop serious problems or become erased. dvds in this area also have mysteriously lost data.

There are other electrical problems in the old section. New light bulbs in new fixtures burn out within a short period of time. Electricians have inspected both the lighting fixtures and the wiring on two occasions and found nothing wrong either time. It was suggested that lower wattage bulbs might work. This change seemed to work for a brief time, but the problem always reoccurred.

It became apparent that the bulbs burning out was not random. There was a pattern. The room containing the four computers in the old Carnegie section starts the pattern, losing two or more lights, then the room called the Carol Renee Lamar Room loses one. Finally, the connecting hall loses one, and then the pattern starts all over again.

Since the problem of burned-out light bulbs in the old section of the library could not be solved, the fixtures are being replaced with fluorescent lighting, which seems to work. However, the phenomenon now has moved to the new section, which had previously been unaffected.

The lights and computers aren't the only unexplained electrical problems. No matter what temperature the staff sets the thermostat in the old library, in the summertime it remains at or near eighty degrees, and the new section thermostat remains near sixty-nine. In the winter the old library thermostat rises to nearly seventy-five degrees and the new library level thermostat rises to nearly seventy degrees.

It's been some time since the director and staff at the Poseyville Carnegie Library have encountered their friendly ghost. However, they now feel that there may be two ghosts. The second is possibly the spirit of a man who evidently enjoyed a pipe from time to time. Occasionally the staff has noticed the smell of fresh pipe tobacco— with no apparent source—near the library reference desk. So far, this ghost has not made itself known in any other way.

Yet there is also the possibility of a third ghost, which is perhaps a poltergeist, or perhaps just the original ghost feeling piqued over some slight. Last August books began turning up in the wrong locations despite repeated attempts at making sure they were properly shelved. Books sometimes fell off their shelves and were found scattered on the floor in the new section or were found shelved upside down.

One morning in October, Campbell arrived at work to find Volume 29 of the Fifteenth Edition of the *New Encyclopedia Britannica* on the floor. This was somewhat baffling to him, since he had locked up the library the previous evening and had, as was his custom, checked for books that had been left on the tables. Where he discovered this volume, he would have had to walk right over it—if not step on it—the night before.

More recently door locks are refusing to unlock. These are new doors installed in 2002 and should still be in excellent condition. The main entrance door in the old library section has been repaired twice, and the lower-level door entrance to the new library section has been repaired once.

Campbell's attempts to photograph the ghosts using a digital camera have been unsuccessful. Nor has anything been captured on the library's four security cameras.

Books being moved or falling, thermostats acting up, light bulbs burning out, computers mysteriously crashing, locks refusing to work—all of these activities have now been joined by additional phenomenon.

The library staff members cannot keep plants alive in the building, no matter how hard they've tried. Any plant brought into the library soon dies. Thus, the library is now decorated with artificial plants.

Recently, another manifestation has occurred on rare occasions: the sounds of heavy footsteps going up the steps from the children's section.

The list of unexplained events taking place in this building seems to go on and on. The library director and staff still feel certain that the ghost or ghosts remain in the library, perhaps watching over the place they enjoyed in life even in death.

Poseyville's library, where the staff has sighted at least one ghost. PHOTO: Stanley M. Campbell

RIPLEY COUNTY

❖❖❖❖❖❖❖❖❖❖ THE COUNTY, NOTED for its furniture and casket industry, was created in 1816, organized in 1818, and named for Maj. Gen. Eleazar Wheellock Ripley (1782–1839), an officer in the War of 1812. Versailles was selected as the county seat in 1818 and named for the French city and palace near Paris.

The 5,903-acre Versailles State Park is the state's second largest. The land was purchased by the National Park Service in 1935, and ownership was passed to Indiana in 1943. Within the park is the four-hundred-foot-long bat cave with ceilings ranging from one to eight feet. A local legend pertaining to this cave concerns a Confederate soldier, a fugitive from Morgan's Raiders who was accepted as a member of a wolf pack that used the cave for their home. As a member of this pack, the soldier lived and hunted with them.

During the Civil War, Versailles was invaded by Morgan's Raiders on July 12, 1863. The troops seized the cash and the citizens' weapons. According to tradition, Morgan's troops stole a collection of jewels stored in the Masonic Lodge. Morgan, being a mason, made his men return the jewels. These can be seen in the Masonic temple on the northwest corner of Tyson and Adams Streets.

Versailles native James Tyson (1856–1941) spent his early years in the printing industry, working in Versailles and Osgood, Indiana. He eventually began traveling throughout the United States and the world. In Chicago, he met and became friends with Charles Walgreen, the founder of Walgreens drugstores. This friendship led Tyson to several positions in the company, from the firm's first bookkeeper to its secretary, following its 1916 incorporation.

Tyson never lost his strong feelings for his hometown. In memory of his mother, in 1937 Tyson designed and built the beautiful and unique Tyson Temple United Methodist Church. The façade of the art deco church is terra cotta. The roof is copper with an aluminum spire. The four-hundred-pound metal front doors open onto beautiful marble floors. The sanctuary is framed by ornate pillars that represent the Taj Mahal, and it includes a beautifully-painted dome ceiling representing an evening autumn sky. Stars were placed in the dome's sky exactly as they were the night his mother died. Not one nail was used to build the church—unbelievable, but true.

Across the street is the Tyson Library, also erected and equipped by Tyson. The exterior was designed with white-glazed brick and a copper roof to harmonize with the church. The library was officially opened on April 30, 1942. Tyson also established the Tyson Waterworks.

The community continues to benefit through Tyson's generosity. In the 1930s he left the church 18,000 shares of Walgreens stock to be distributed to the community every September 14, his birthday. Those shares have multiplied. By 2002 the endowment was estimated to be between $18 and $21 million. Many residents have benefited from Tyson's gift of love for his hometown of Versailles.

Batesville owes its existence to the routing of the Lawrenceburg to Indianapolis railroad through the northern part of Ripley County. The town was laid out in 1852 by Joshua Bates, a railroad engineer.

The large supply of timber in the area attracted mainly Germans, mostly from Cincinnati. They began Batesville's primary industry of woodworking. By 1900 six furniture factories, two coffin and casket plants, two sawmills, and a door and sash factory existed in the town.

Four generations of Batesville's Hillenbrand family have been community leaders. They were one of the pioneer furniture-making families who settled in the town. Their business began with a general store in the 1870s, but subsequently they created the American Furniture Company in the 1880s, and later the Batesville Casket Company in 1906, and the Batesville Cabinet Company years later.

Today Hillenbrand Industries Inc. includes Hill-Rom, manufacturers of hospital furniture; the Forethought Group, an insurance firm; and the Batesville Casket Company, which produces one-fifth of the world's caskets.

At the northwest corner of Main and George Streets is the Sherman House, an historic hostelry dating from 1852. Its popularity has long been known among travelers because of its excellent cuisine and convenient location between Cincinnati and Indianapolis.

The city of Milan was laid out by David Brooks in 1854. The high point of Milan's history took place in 1954. Not only did the tiny town celebrate its centennial, but its high school won the state basketball championship by beating Muncie Central 32–30. The final two-point shot was executed by Bobby Plump, who received the coveted Arthur L. Trester Award and was named Indiana's "Mr. Basketball."

Milan was the inspiration for the 1986 movie š š shot in Indiana and starring Gene Hackman, Barbara Hershey, and Dennis Hopper, who was nominated for an Oscar. David Anspaugh, a Decatur, Indiana, native, directed the picture, and Angelo Pizzo, Anspaugh's former roommate at Indiana University, wrote and co-produced it. ❖

The Wolf Man

In 1863, Gen. John Hunt Morgan's Raiders entered Indiana intent on raiding Union supplies and creating general panic. As they neared Versailles one of the Confederate soldiers, for reasons only known to him, deserted his unit and made his way into the woods.

His strange story has become one of southern Indiana's many folktales. Throughout the years the story has been repeated, and he was given the name of Silas Shimmerhorn.

The soldier made his home in the wilderness surrounding Versailles, eventually taking up residence in a cave known today as Bat Cave, located within the boundaries of Versailles State Park.

He had his rifle and ammunition and used these to hunt for food until the ammunition was gone. Continuing the effort to find food, he set traps for rabbits and birds. Some say he even ventured out under the cover of darkness to forage in the fields and steal chickens and eggs from the farmers.

His greatest fear was discovery either by Morgan or the citizens. In either case he was certain he'd be killed. As food became increasingly difficult to obtain, the additional fear of starvation weighed heavily on his mind.

Another fear manifested itself in the form of a pack of wild wolves who laid claim to the area around his cave home. At first he didn't realize he had nothing to fear from these predators. He was wary of them but respectful, and in turn they treated him in the same manner. Thus, man and predator existed side-by-side.

The legend surrounding the man and the wolves tells of his joining the pack as it raided farms, killing chickens, cows, and pigs. It's believed he had fashioned a crude bow and arrows, and that during these nighttime attacks would kill many of the animals the wolves and he shared. The farmers began noticing strange wounds on the carcasses of their animals. Beside the telltale signs of wolves' teeth, there were unexplained puncture wounds, and many of the animals bore signs of a knife being used to butcher the meat.

Farmers began staying up at night with their shotguns loaded and aimed at their fields in hopes of protecting their animals and killing a few wolves. They weren't prepared for what they began encountering during their vigils. Reports started circulating that a man was seen running wild with the marauding wolf pack. He was described as wearing no shirt or shoes. He had long flowing hair and beard.

On several occasions the farmers tried to catch the Wolf Man, but he was far too cunning. The wolves had taught him well. Eventually they were able to track him to his hiding place—the Bat Cave—where they were met by snarls and snapping teeth as the wolf pack protected the entrance. Out of fear for their lives, the farmers retreated.

The Wolf Man and his pack continued to raid farms and evade capture. Bounties were placed on the wolves, and soon the area was rid of the problem. The Wolf Man seemed to disappear as well. His story became just that—a story, one that people loved to tell, to believe or disbelieve. After several years, a group of farmers decided to visit the Bat Cave and see what they could find.

According to the stories, they did find what they described as the remnants of a straw bed and a rifle. Etched on the stock were the initials "S.S." There was no sign of Silas Shimmerhorn, though. No bones. Nothing.

The stories continued to be told, but they were not always believed. After all, they were just stories. But many years after the farmers visited the cave, there were reported sightings of a wolf pack running through a field, in its midst a man with long flowing hair and a beard. As the pack ran toward the woods the moonlight gave them an eerie otherworldly glow. Once they entered the woods and were out of sight, the air was filled with the echoing howls of man and beasts.

It is believed that the ghosts of the Wolf Man and his friends, the wolves, still haunt the Versailles State Park. Even when they're not seen, their howls can still be heard in the night.

SPENCER COUNTY

❖❖❖❖❖❖❖❖❖❖ THIS COUNTY is famous as the place where Abraham Lincoln spent his formative years (1816–1830). The county was organized in 1818 and named for Capt. Spier Spencer, who was killed in the Battle of Tippecanoe.

Rockport was settled in 1802 and first called Hanging Rock, for the projecting rock formations. Five years later the name was changed to Mount Duvall for Col. William Duvall. When the city was chosen as the county seat in 1818, the name was changed to Rockport. Today Rockport is the county's largest town and commercial seat. Rockport has had its share of notables either born or raised within its limits. Two of these are Kate Milner Rabb, author and columnist for the *Indianapolis News* and Florence Henderson, star of stage, screen, and television.

The Lincoln Pioneer Village & Museum is located in Rockport City Park. The vintage and replica log homes, along with their contents, was assembled during 1934 and 1935. The village contains accurate representations of the inn, church, school, law office, store, homes, and many other buildings significant to Lincoln's life during the fourteen years he lived in Indiana. In 1954 the village served as a backdrop for part of the movie *The Kentuckian*, starring Burt Lancaster. The movie's production crew erected a structure depicting an early tobacco warehouse. Today this building is used as a transportation museum with several buggies, a hearse, and other horse-drawn vehicles on display.

Lincoln City was platted in 1872—on land that once be-longed to Abraham Lincoln's father, Thomas—and named for the family. Today, it is the site of the Lincoln

Boyhood National Memorial, the family's original log cabin, Lincoln's mother's grave, and the Lincoln family cemetery. Across the road is Lincoln State Park, where you can enjoy a musical drama titled *Young Abe Lincoln* at the outdoor, covered 1,500-seat Lincoln Amphitheater.

Another notable Spencer County location is Saint Meinrad Archabbey, which was founded in 1854 and is the present-day home of Abbey Press. The press produces many religious publications and gift items, which are for sale in their gift shop. ✤

The Mathias Sharp House

In November 2001 I received a message from Vevah Harris, Spencer County Visitors' Bureau, in Santa Claus, Indiana. She had heard I was interested in information on haunted spots in that county. "The Mathias Sharp House in Rockport, Indiana, is an old mansion located on a bluff overlooking the Ohio River," she told me. "The widow who once lived there lost two husbands from 'food poisoning.' Coincidence? Perhaps. Anyway, the house is supposed to be haunted. This property is privately owned; but there is a historic marker in the yard telling about the widow and the poisoned husbands."

She definitely got my attention.

The story begins at Rockport in the 1800s. Mathias Sharp was a successful farmer, beekeeper, and hog raiser. He and his wife worked hard for their family and looked forward to a comfortable life after the children had left the homestead. Unfortunately, his wife became ill and died. Several years passed. The general prosperity of the 1850s necessitated a new plank road. About this time Sharp's last child left home. Mathias, it was said, took part in many of the community's projects, including acting as a part-time supervisor on the construction of the plank road. One day, as he was surveying the construction of a new covered bridge, he lost his footing and fell.

The workers took him to the nearest farmer's house where the daughter, Katherine, administered to his needs while he waited for the doctor. No bones were broken, but he had sustained a severe sprain and would need nursing. Katherine, it seems, had helped nurse Mathias's wife before her death, and thus he felt comfortable having her come to his house to assist him.

By the late 1860s the two were married. However, the home where he and his first wife had lived was not suitable to Katherine. She wanted her own. Mathias hired a contractor to build a new home on the edge of the bluffs, high above the Ohio River.

It was 1867, and the house was nearing completion when it became apparent that Mathias would have to sell some of his acreage to cover the bill. Katherine also was not content with using the furniture that had been her predecessor's and insisted on new and expensive furniture. Mathias bowed to his wife's desires, and once again it became necessary to sell more of his land. His children were not very happy about the diminishing of what they felt was their inheritance.

One evening as Mathias and Katherine ate supper in their new home, Mathias became ill, went into convulsions, and died. His children were convinced that Katherine had poisoned him. Could she have also expedited his first wife's death? This was rumored to be a possibility, but was never investigated. Mathias's death was also never officially investigated.

Sometime during the building of the bluff house, Mr. Batchelor, a merchant, came to town. It wasn't long after Sharp's death that Katherine and Batchelor became friends and eventually married, and he moved into Katherine's house on the bluff.

During supper one evening, Batchelor, sitting at the same table in the same chair that Mathias had sat in before his death, became ill. He too, went into convulsions and died.

Once again, Mathias Sharp's children demanded something be done. They were certain Katherine had poisoned another husband.

They were able to block Batchelor's burial and also have their own father exhumed. Tests were performed to determine the cause of death in both cases. Sharp's children had been correct: Both men died of arsenic poisoning.

Katherine was indicted and prosecuted for the poisoning of both husbands. It could not have been anyone else, for in both cases only Katherine prepared the meals and could have easily added arsenic to the food. The prosecutor was certain that the jury, based on the evidence, would find Katherine guilty. But when the jury retired to deliberate and decide Katherine's fate, and regardless of the evidence against her, she was acquitted!

That evening the prosecutor was discussing the case with the judge, and he learned that the judge had given the jury some unique instructions before the deliberation—instructions that re-flected his distrust of the findings of the "scientific men." He told the prosecutor, "I wasn't going to have a woman hanged just because of what a damned expert with a kettleful of guts said." He then added, "That woman is my neighbor—I keep my cows in her pasture."

Although Katherine was acquitted, she lost her home to Capt. Eigenman, a prominent Rockport businessman who had loaned her the money to pay for her defense. In 1877 Dr. Carl H. Eigenman lived in the house with his uncle, Capt. Eigenman. For approximately thirteen years after that, it was rented for brief periods but mainly remained unoccupied. Later the property was purchased by the Posey family. Just before and during their occupancy was when the haunting tales began.

In 1916 a correspondent for the *Rockport Courier* recounted some of these tales.

When the reporter asked one of the women in the community if she'd heard anything about the haunting, the woman said, "Oh, yes! There's lots of stories about the old house that we girls loved to tell on Halloween nights and at our ghost parties. The one I remember best and one my mother, along with many others of the older residents, believed thoroughly, is that about crashing glass being heard on wedding nights."

Then the woman shared the story of newlyweds who'd just moved into the Sharp home. On the dining table they'd displayed their wedding gifts, including a beautiful cut-glass water set. The wife was concerned about keeping this expensive gift out during the night, but her husband assured her it would be safe and that he'd make certain all the doors and windows were locked.

The couple no sooner had fallen asleep when they were awoken by the sound of breaking glass. They rushed into the dining room to find their beautiful cut glass shattered. After a quick check through the house, the husband reported that all the doors and windows were still locked. There was no other explanation for the glass being broken other than the house was haunted! The couple soon moved out.

As the story goes, two other newlywed couples who rented the home experienced similar events. They, too, beat a hasty retreat from the haunted house.

The *Evansville Courier* article conveyed yet another eerie legend. A white bird with a bell tied around its neck appeared at the house every night for one year. It could be seen perched on the chimney. This was a good omen. Many of the help employed by the family believed this indicated someone in the house would marry. This belief came to pass when one of the hired girls married. After that, the white bird with the "wedding" bell disappeared.

Then a black bird, "as black as coal," appeared. Unlike the white bird it had no bell, but it "made a terrible mournful" sound all the time. Soon after the appearance of this bird, the lady of the house died.

When the Poseys moved into the house, they laughed at the many stories they had heard. They hadn't personally experienced anything that would make them believe the house was haunted.

One summer after the Poseys moved in, there was an occurrence that led them to believe otherwise. One afternoon Mrs. Posey and her daughters watched from the porch as an odd figure in a long black dress came slowly up the driveway. As the figure came near the porch, they heard her say, "They robbed me of this place. They robbed me of this place." The woman walked silently around the house and then, just as mysteriously as she appeared, she was gone. The Posey family did not believe that this was a ghost; instead, they chose to believe that it was the aging Katherine in the flesh. Was it?

In this home that the infamous Katherine once owned—and, some say, still roams in her spectral form—she could assume only squatter's rights. On October 31, 1982, Sylvia Slaughter, the *Evansville Courier & Press* Sunday Feature Editor, wrote an article about the continued haunting of the Mathias Sharp home. At the time of this article, the house was owned by Garrett Wilkinson and his family.

The Wilkinsons were aware of Katherine's story when they moved into the house with their two children. They were often stopped on the streets by Rockport citizens who complimented them on their efforts to bring the house back from the neglected state it had fallen into. But more often it was to tell them ghost stories about their house. The parents were not concerned and considered the stories to be just a conversation piece. However, their teenage son, Garth, admitted to the reporter that he'd seen "one ghost in the house." It was not Katherine. It was a man. Could it have been one of her murdered husbands?

Today it is owned by the Marsh family. Although they like their privacy, their house has become a bit of a tourist attraction. Rockport

residents bring friends from far and near to see their legendary "haunted" house at 319 South Second Street.

Historic Marker outside of the Mathais Sharp House. PHOTO: Vevah Harris, Spencer County Visitor's Bureau

SULLIVAN COUNTY

❖❖❖❖❖❖❖❖❖❖❖ THE COUNTY, organized in 1817, was named for Daniel Sullivan, a Revolutionary War hero who was killed while carrying messages from Vincennes to Louisville. The county seat of Sullivan was platted in 1842 and named for the county. The city of Sullivan was the home of movie czar Will H. Hays (1879–1954), who was head of the Motion Picture Producers and Distributors of America (1922–1945). He also had been chairman of the Republican National Committee (1918–1921) and post-master general for President Warren G. Harding (1921–1922). Of significance to women's history in Sullivan is a plaque erected in 1937 in the Sullivan Courthouse Rotunda. It honors Sullivan attorney Antoinette Leach, who in 1893 became the first woman to be admitted to the Indiana bar.

The town of Hymera, originally named Merom, was platted in 1879.

In the Bethel Cemetery is a ten-foot-tall statue of a Revo-lutionary War soldier at parade, resting atop a five-foot-tall base that marks the gravesite of Nathan Hinkle. Born in 1749, Hinkle enlisted in the Pennsylvania militia in 1776, serving seven years. He later moved west to Sullivan County, where he died in 1848 at the age of ninety-nine years and six months.

Within Sullivan County is the Shakamak State Park. The name is a Kickapoo Indian term meaning "river of the long fish" for the Eel River that runs through the local area. The park also has three lakes. Established in 1929 on the site of strip mines, the park is an example of the efforts of the state and coal industry to reclaim strip-mined land.

The earliest settlement in the county was Carlisle. A Revolutionary War veteran, James Ledgerwood and his

family settled here in 1803. The town was officially platted in 1815 by his son, Samuel. From 1817 to 1819, Carlisle
served as the first county seat until it was decided
Merom would be a more likely site for the government
based on its location on the busy Wabash River. The
county seat was eventually moved to Sullivan in 1942.

With the arrival of the railroad in 1850, Carlisle developed into a shipping center. On the town square is a
marker commemorating a Revolutionary War naval skir-
mish, the only one fought in Indiana, which took place at
a site eight miles northwest of the town at a double bend
in the Wabash River. The Americans won the battle capturing seven boats, forty men, and supplies. ❖

The Ferree (Free) Springs Bridge Ghosts

Some believe that bridges are more than spans across water: They
can be used by spirits as a bridge between our world and theirs.
Just southeast of the town of Sullivan there are two such bridges
believed to be used by both the living and the spirits of the
de-parted. To find these bridges as you near Sullivan, take Center
Road West from the 41 bypass. Turn left on to County Road 175-
West and continue for about a half-mile to the bottom of the hill
and across the railroad tracks.

You will arrive in the area where the spirits walk. To your right
will be a railroad trestle, you'll see a bridge straight ahead, and just
upstream and to the west will be Ferree Springs. The springs,
which feed into Buck Creek, are named for early landowners.

Many people in this area believe that the Ferree Springs Bridge
is haunted. There have been reports of strange sounds as well as
sightings of a headless ghost. Area youth often visit the site at
night hoping to catch a glimpse of what haunts the area.

One legend concerns a "knight of the road" who used to ride on the front platform of a train, between the last car and the caboose. One night as the train crossed the trestle, the man fell from the platform. He landed with his head positioned on the track. The last set of wheels left him decapitated. His body fell into the stream and came to rest under the Ferree Springs Bridge.

His head was never found. There were no identifying papers on the body, and no one stepped forward claim it. Thus, his headless corpse was buried unceremoniously in an unmarked grave.

Just a few days after his death and burial, people traveling the road near the bridge began reporting strange sounds and sightings. Stories began circulating that the ghost of the man would not rest until it found its head. Passers-by would claim to see a headless man walking the bridge and the trestle. Many reported that there was a light about the man as if he was carrying a lantern, while others said it was the ghost itself glowing. Some claimed they'd seen the disembodied head floating in air—but the body and the head never met. Both are said to still be haunting the area.

There's another ghost that is said to haunt this area. Some time ago a young man and his girlfriend were returning home from a date, when their car suddenly careened off the road, crashed into a tree, and burst into flames.

What had caused this accident? The weather wasn't bad. Could he have seen the headless ghost or the head floating in front of his car? The young man was evidently thrown clear of the car. Yet he seemed to have disappeared, for no body was found. There was no sign of him. Had he survived and wandered off in a daze? His girlfriend was not so lucky. She died in the inferno.

A year later on the anniversary of the accident, people passing by the bridge reported hearing a male's voice—seemingly coming from nowhere—calling the name of the girl who'd died.

On the anniversary of the fiery crash people still report hearing the young man's voice in the night calling out her name. But that can't be. It was far too long ago. He could not have outlived time. Unless, of course, he's only a ghost of the man he once was.

VANDERBURGH COUNTY

❖❖❖❖❖❖❖❖❖❖❖THIS COUNTY, ONE OF Indiana's smallest in area, was organized in 1818 and named for Judge Henry Vanderburgh (1760–1812), a New York native who presided over the Northwest Territory Legislative Council in 1799 and served on the first Board of Trustees of Vincennes University.

Evansville, the county seat, is Indiana's fourth largest city. The town was named for Gen. Robert Evans. Because of its proximity to the Ohio River, railroads, and Louisville, Evansville is an important point of transportation. The community also dominates the economic and cultural life of southwest Indiana, western Kentucky, and Illinois.

During the Civil War, the city was a major contributor and conduit of troops and provisions. From the county came more than three thousand Union army enlistees, including nine-year-old drummer boy John W. Messick, reportedly the youngest Union recruit.

Paul Dresser (1859–1906), author of Indiana's state song, "On the Banks of the Wabash Far Away" (1897), lived in Evansville in the 1880s. Living with him for a short time were his mother and several siblings, including Theodore Dreiser (Paul Americanized the surname), who became one of the most celebrated Indiana-born authors.

With the passage of liquor prohibition laws, organized bootlegging operations capitalized on Evansville's lo-cation on the Ohio River, shuttling the illegal item between Kentucky and Indiana. From the south came the Ku Klux Klan in 1920. D.C. Stephenson began his meteoric rise in the Klan in the Evansville area. Soon he became Indiana's Grand Dragon and a power in state politics until his downfall in 1926.

The Angel Mounds State Historic Site is the home of a 103-acre Middle Mis-sissippian Indian village and trade center, dating back to 1100–1450 A.D. About one thousand people lived in the village's thatched-roofed houses surrounded by a stockade. Eleven communal buildings were constructed on earthen mounds. In the 1930s the threat of loosing this unique archeological area was called to the attention of Eli Lilly, who purchased the site from the Angel family and others. From 1939 to 1942, a team of archaeologists headed by Glenn A. Black conducted systematic excavations. Some 2.3 million items turned up during the three years of research and reconstruction. An Interpretive Center was constructed in 1972, featuring a simulated excavation and exhibits of Indian material culture. Exact replicas of family dwellings, ceremonial structures, and a stockade section have been added. ❖

Raining Stones

On Thursday, August 7, 1952, the Associated Press carried a story datelined Evansville and captioned "Rocks From 'No-where' Still Falling." The story stated that in the night, stones had been raining down on the Chattins' family-owned filling station and restaurant, seven miles north of Evansville, at the intersection of u.s. Route 41 and Old State Road. This phenomenon had been going on for a week with no indications that it was going to stop.

Three families lived very close to this building, and though they experienced some of the rain of stones, it was quite obvious the target was the filling station and restaurant.

Two deputy sheriffs had been dispatched to the area, but they had been baffled and were unable to determine the cause. As word got out, people began gathering as the sky darkened, waiting and watching. A few curious ones even picked up some of the stones as soon as they dropped to the ground; they reported that they were warm to the touch. Still no one had an answer.

One individual interviewed said he wasn't surprised by the strange event, since this was "Dutch" country and anything could and had happened in the area. He told the story of an old woman near Madisonville who had died. After her death a tree in her yard had twisted into a shape that resembled the old woman. Postcards were made of this tree and thousands had been sold.

Photographers from *Life* magazine arrived on the scene to take pictures of the stones. The owners of the building had collected buckets full of these rocks and joked that they probably could retire if they sold them to the curious, since "people were such fools."

The stones began falling at dusk and continued sporadically until one or two o'clock in the morning. Sometimes only one or two rocks would fall each hour, and at other times, they would fall like a spring rain, pelting the building and even breaking windows. However, most of the stones were no larger than pebbles and appeared to be white limestone.

The deputies dispatched to the site enlisted members of the families living nearby and even some members of the curious crowd to search the area for the cause—in the hope of either frightening the "vandals" or capturing them. It was widely believed the culprits were teenagers. Volunteers searched diligently night and day throughout a half-mile area surrounding the building. A wooded area just east of the building and parallel to *U.S.* Route 41 was considered to be the most likely site for some sort of homemade slingshot capable of hurling the stones, but nothing was found.

The deputies continued to protect the building and the area, but by the fifth night even their cars had been targeted. The next night the deputies and several volunteers hid in the woods and tall grass, determined to catch the hoodlums. Meanwhile, the little restaurant's business had picked up considerably; the curious who came night after night would order several cups of coffee and hamburgers, and wait for the next rain of stones.

One old weather-beaten local, who had watched this strange experience with the others every night, expressed the belief that it was ghosts throwing the rocks. He said he believed in ghosts because he had seen many in his time.

Usually, the stones would come down as if they were being dropped from a cloud, but sometimes they would come at an angle whereby they would hit the sides of the building and some of the cars parked nearby. After a period of perhaps an hour or two, the deluge would seem to stop and everyone would enter the restaurant for more coffee—but then the rain of stones would begin plinking on the roof. Sometimes the following rain would consist of smaller stones than before, about the size of peas.

Many theories were expressed as to where the stones were coming from—teenagers, meteorites, volcanic eruptions. (Volcanoes in Indiana?) All of these theories were disproved. But we must not forget the old man's theory. Could the culprits have been ghosts?

Oscar the Friendly Ghost

Oscar's story begins in 1922. The kids in Oscar's Evansville neighborhood knew him as a friendly, outgoing nineteen-year-old who took delight in giving them rides in his car. They would pile in, eager to careen over the dusty roads around the city. Late in the evening Oscar would bring them back to his house, and, calling their goodnights, they would scatter to their own homes.

The routine didn't vary that one evening in the early 1920s when everyone waved as Oscar went into his house. They never saw him again. His parents found him dead in bed the next morning.

The house where Oscar lived and died, at 611 Harriet Street, is gone now. The lot is occupied by a medical clinic. But back in 1942, Gladys and Warren Reynolds, a young married couple, lived in what was once Oscar's home and became friends with his spirit.

At first, Gladys Reynolds thought she was hearing ordinary

noises, the settling and maturing sounds heard in many homes. Her husband, however, felt from the beginning that there was something different about the sounds.

Gladys worked days, and her husband, a deputy sheriff, worked nights. Oscar seemed to be around more during the day when Warren was home. He'd hear the sounds, and also began to experience or sense activity that was not human—but it wasn't frightening or malicious either.

The Reynolds's first real indication that Oscar was still in "his" house came during a thunderstorm. The family was in a downstairs room, when suddenly they heard footsteps running across the upstairs hall. Then they heard what sounded like windows being shut in the bedrooms. When the family checked, each window that had been open was now closed against the brewing storm.

Oscar was apparently a shy ghost who preferred to be heard and not seen. On only two occasions did he allow himself to be seen— both times by Warren Reynolds's mother who lived with her son and daughter-in-law until her death. During her stay she occupied the same bedroom believed to have been Oscar's.

Late one night she was awakened by a sharp sound. Looking around the room, she saw a shadowy male figure, which she took to be Oscar, standing with his back to her, bending over the fireplace grate. Hoping the specter would disappear, the old woman pulled the blankets over her head. Oscar finally melted into the darkness.

His next visit was a bit shorter, and again took place at night. He was standing quite still next to a potted plant with his back toward Mrs. Reynolds, who had once again been awakened from a sound sleep. And, as before, after a few seconds he seemed to melt away.

Although he was seldom seen, the Reynolds family always knew when Oscar was around. He seemed to like the cane-bottomed rocker. The family often heard its familiar creaking when they knew the room was empty.

Oscar also liked to prowl about the partially-finished attic. One afternoon the husband heard someone walking about. He thought some kids had broken in through a window. Since he was a deputy sheriff, he took out his revolver and headed up the stairs. But when he got there, he couldn't find anything. All the windows were locked and nothing had been disturbed. He was certain, though, that he'd heard someone—or what used to be someone—walking around.

In 1948 a friend of Gladys's came to visit for a few days. Late on the first evening after her friend had retired, Gladys heard sounds coming from upstairs like drawers opening and closing. Then she heard footsteps and doors shutting. She thought perhaps her friend had suddenly changed her mind and was preparing to leave early in the morning. The next morning at breakfast her friend assured her that she was staying and that she had slept throughout the night, never once getting out of bed.

The Reynolds family moved out of Oscar's house in 1965. Oscar, however, may have been so attached to the family that he moved with them into their next home. They told friends and family that at times they'd hear faint footsteps or the creaking of the rocking chair Oscar had fancied. And there were at least two occasions when objects mysteriously disappeared, only to be found later in places the family had thoroughly searched. Gladys and Warren attributed these incidents to pranks pulled by Oscar. You could say he was just one of the family.

The Gray Lady of Willard Library

Evansville's Willard Library is described as the oldest working library in Indiana. The two-story library was built in 1885 on land donated by Willard Carpenter, who also financed its construction. It is a showcase of Italian Gothic architecture with a Victorian corner tower—and a ghost.

The ghost is known as the Lady in Gray. She first made herself known in 1937, when a janitor encountered her as he went downstairs to stoke the building's furnace. It was his custom to go to the building very early in the morning to shovel more coal into the furnace to get the library warm for the morning opening.

He'd arrived, as usual, entering the unlit basement with his flashlight trained on the floor so he wouldn't stumble. As he neared the furnace, he raised his flashlight. The beam revealed a lady dressed in gray. He was so startled he dropped the light. As he bent down to pick it up, he noticed that even her shoes were gray. Just as suddenly as she'd appeared in the halo of light, the image dissolved into the shadows. The janitor wasn't able to describe her face because it had been covered by a gray veil. Needless to say, the janitor quit.

A new janitor was hired, but was not informed of his predecessor's ghostly encounter. Early on his first morning he entered the basement to stoke the furnace. He completed his chore and was turning around when he bumped into something—something that felt human, or almost human. Taking a step backward and training his flashlight at the object, he saw a lady dressed in gray from the top of her head to her shoes. Then she disappeared. The janitor left and never returned.

The lady continues to be very active. There are numerous reports of shadows scurrying in the library's basement, which at one time housed the children's room before it was moved upstairs. Once these rooms were in their new location, librarians reported books falling off the shelves for no apparent reason. One librarian stated that she'd been alone in the children's room when someone, or something, pulled back her hair and touched her earring. On several occasions, there have been reports of water being mysteriously turned on throughout the building. Also, lights have been turned on or off, but by no human hand. Several people have reported the scent of a strong fragrance floating past them. And, from time to time, she's been seen just standing and watching.

One of the first reports of anyone smelling her fragrance happened one night when two staff members stayed late to complete microfilming (appropriately enough) cemetery records. One worker went into the restroom and became aware of a very heavy perfume. No one else was in the room, and she was not wearing any fragrance.

Although the Lady in Gray wonders about the library she seems to enjoy the children's room most of all. The librarians often hear scurrying feet when they open the doors to that room. Beginning in the late 1950s, the ghost evidently became very fond of one of the children's librarians, Margaret Maier. Margaret stayed alone late one night in the library. Or was she alone? Suddenly, she heard the sound of water running in a sink on the second floor. The faucet had mysteriously turned itself on. Later, the gray lady made herself visible to Margaret and her assistant. Both employees saw her standing by the refrigerator in the staff room.

The library began a renovation project in 1980 that involved the children's area. Margaret reported that she believed the lady had gone home with her during this renovation. One night she and her sister, Ruth, were alone in their house when they both experienced a draft of cold air and the feeling of a presence that was followed by the scent of strong perfume.

There were other strange happenings in the sisters' home. They reported watching the ghost moving about the house from the darkened dining room to the lighted living room. They saw her so plainly that they were able to describe her dress. It appeared to be made of wool and had long pleats in the skirt. While the Lady in Gray stayed at their home she never wore her veil.

In 1997, a spokesperson for the library said that the lady is still very much a part of the building, reporting a story of a woman and her family who had recently moved to Evansville and were in the library for the first time. As they began climbing the steps to the second floor, the woman turned to her husband and said, "Bob, there's somebody on the steps with us." They both turned, and just behind them, they saw the shadowy figure of a woman dressed in gray. Be-fore their eyes she seemed to melt away. Another sighting was reported to the director in August of that year. A male staff member was on the second floor at the end of an aisle, near a back corner, when he suddenly felt cold. He felt compelled to look around the corner. To his surprise, he came face to face with the gray lady, who he described as being transparent. They stood looking at each other for a few seconds before she disappeared.

Many who have visited the library or who have watched the library's online ghost camera still report experiences or sightings.

But who is the lady? Could she be the ghost of Louise Carpenter, a daughter of Willard Carpenter, the man who founded the library? Louise was very unhappy at the money her father left the library and, some years after his death, sued to have his will revoked on grounds of insanity. She failed and became a very bitter lady. Willard's Lady in Gray is a shy and gentle ghost. Many believe that if the ghost was Louise, she would be mean and angry.

Others believe that the lady has no connections with the library itself. They think that she belongs to the park that was there before the library was built. According to legend, a woman and her son were in the park when he fell into a small pond and drowned. The pond was filled in, and the library was built over the area. Many believe that she is still searching for her son.

Greg Hager, director of the Willard Library, responded when asked whether he ever dreamed that he would be the director of a haunted library, "No. I didn't know that I would be doing PR for a ghost."

Printed in the USA
CPSIA information can be obtained
at www.ICGtesting.com
JSHW011036260124
55823JS00003B/8